FEEDING TOMMY

This book is dedicated to the memory of army cooks such as Private G/12022 Abel Flitney, who died of wounds in the Battle of Passchendaele on 2 August 1917, and to all cooks who served and made the supreme sacrifice in the Great War.

FEEDING TOMMY

BATTLEFIELD RECIPES
FROM THE FIRST WORLD WAR

ANDREW ROBERTSHAW

IN ASSOCIATION WITH THE ROYAL LOGISTIC CORPS MUSEUM

First published 2013
by Spellmount, an imprint of The History Press
The Mill, Brimscombe Port
Stroud, Gloucestershire, GL5 2QG
www.thehistorypress.co.uk

British Library Cataloguing in Publication Data.
A catalogue record for this book is available from the British Library.

ISBN 978 0 7524 8875 2

Typesetting and origination by The History Press
Printed in Great Britain
Manufacturing managed by Jellyfish Solutions Ltd

CONTENTS

ACKNOWLEDGEMENTS

FOR MANY PEOPLE rations in the Great War have been summed up by a conversation in the famous television series *Blackadder Goes Forth*, which ran from 1983 to 1989. When Captain Edmund Blackadder, who is serving in the trenches of the First World War, asks what there is to eat, his soldier servant, Private Baldrick, replies:

> Private Baldrick: 'Rat au Van, Sir.'
> Captain Blackadder: 'Rat au Van, Baldrick?'
> Private Baldrick: 'Yes Sir, it's rat that's been…'
> Captain Blackadder: 'Run over by a van.'[1]

Without wishing to dismiss in any way the humour of the piece, the fact that the *Blackadder Goes Forth* series is now included as a source in the curriculum about the First World War indicates that this exchange represents a common view of trench rations. A quick survey of resources for schools on the Internet produced the following (the emphasis is my own):

> By the time the food reached the frontline it was *always* cold.

> Eventually the army moved the field kitchens closer to the frontline but they were *never* able to get close enough to provide regular hot food for the men.

> Men claimed that although the officers were well-fed the men in the trenches were *treated appallingly.*

I am grateful for the opportunity to present the reality based on the archives of The Royal Logistic Corps Museum and a range of contemporary accounts by the men who cooked the rations and ate them between 1914 and 1918. This book is interspersed with hints and tips that they learnt during service and their recipes, kindly reproduced courtesy of the Trustees of The Royal Logistic Corps Museum.

I would like to express my thanks to the many army 'chefs', as they are now called, who have supported The Royal Logistic Corps Museum and myself with this project.

PREFACE

WHETHER IT IS a memorable meal when out of the trenches or the failure of the rations to arrive on a cold wet morning in the frontline, descriptions of life on the Western Front are littered with references to food. To those who read the accounts, soldiers appear obsessed by food. Whether soldiers are in the frontline as infantrymen, serving the guns, driving vehicles or caring for animals, they need to eat. Even if the men who had been civilians before the war and now found themselves in 'the ranks' had not always eaten adequate meals in civil life, they expected to be paid for their military service and to receive 'three square meals' a day. Many of the recruits of 1914 enlisted to get new clothes on their backs, rations to eat, regular pay and to 'do their bit'. For many in a world before the welfare state, and at the time of an economic recession, the imperative of food and the promise of meals, not love of King and Country, brought them to the recruiting office. It was noticed by many instructors and officers that recruits rapidly filled out. Younger ones even put on stature as a response to the rations they received, combined with exercise and unaccustomed physical activity.

Soldiers are often young men, who are both growing and involved in strenuous activity. In consequence, they are frequently constantly hungry and sometimes looking for comfort in what can be a bleak environment with little other opportunity for enjoyment. A soldier serving as a transport driver with the London Rifle Brigade states in his memoir:

> It was a curious thing that when food was in abundance, as on lines of communication, we did not possess enormous appetites; but when we had ... half-slices of bread, estimating we couldn't eat more now because we should have to want a little for the next meal ... we seemed suddenly to have a craving for twice as much as we normally ate.[2]

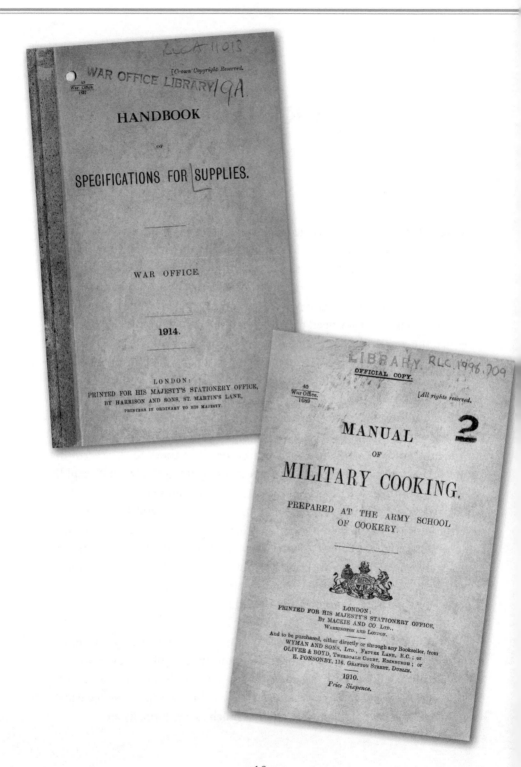

If older soldiers were not so hungry, they appear to search for food that is familiar and reminds them of home; this, potentially, provides a break from the tedium of military rations, in which the diner has no choice of menu. Whether it was the pure satisfaction of eating or the search for variety that compelled soldiers, they all knew that meals were critical. This was recognised by the army and throughout the war the military authorities did all that could be done to ensure adequate and well-cooked rations were available. Hungry men make bad soldiers, hence the axiom attributed to Napoleon: 'An Army marches on its stomach'.

Although the Great War of popular imagination has soldiers constantly underfed and virtually begging for food, the reality is rather different. In the autumn of 1914, Private Frank Richards records:

> There was no such things as cooked food or hot tea at this stage of the war, and the rations were very scarce, we were lucky if we got our four biscuits a man daily, a pound tin of 'bully' between two, a tin of jam between six and the rum ration which was about a tablespoon and a half.[3]

This describes the early phase of trench warfare before the supply chain to the United Kingdom and Empire was fully established and before local purchase became common. Despite these advances, there could be local problems during periods of shelling, combat or movement of units. Private Beatson recalled an occasion in the trenches when there was no food at all: 'The following day we had no rations sent us, our "emergencies" were done, and the men went hungry'.[4] In extreme circumstances, as George Coppard makes clear, casualties could provide a bonus for men in an emergency: 'Gruesome and distasteful as it was, we augmented our supplies from the dead ... a tin of bully in a dead man's pack can't help him, nor can a pack of cigarettes. Many a good smoke came our way in this manner.'[5] A soldier of the London Rifle Brigade describes a situation in 1915, in which 'No rations arrive, I opened my haversack and pulled out a tin of bully beef, two biscuits and some tea leaves, on which I proceeded to make a breakfast'.[6] He also notes the effect that even a hot drink could have, however it was prepared: 'For tea, Bourke and Whittle heated a mug full of cocoa over two candles and shared the drink with Thomson and me. Three sips of this worked wonders'.[7] Sometimes the shortage of food was the result of

11

official policy and right at the end of the war, on 11 November 1918, an unknown non-commissioned officer (NCO) of the Royal Army Medical Corps (RAMC), who was supervising a hospital ward, announced that, 'To celebrate the conclusion of hostilities every patient will be allowed an extra piece of bread and jam with his tea'.[8]

George Coppard provides a balance of attitude towards the matter of rations. Out of the frontline his view was that, 'The cooking arrangements were good too. "Burgoo" (porridge) before the breakfast fry-up, and "spotted dog" (currant pudding) with dinner, were welcome fillers'.[9] However, conditions in the frontline were a contrast:

> Sharing out the rations for a small unit was a bit of a lottery, especially where tins of jam, bully beef, pork and beans, butter and so on were concerned. The share-out was seldom favourable to a six-man team. So far as I know there were no hard and fast rules regarding the quantity of each type of ration a man was entitled to. The Army Service Corps [ASC] were the main distributors, but how much food actually arrived in the trenches depended on such things as transport, the weather and enemy action. Irregular appropriations were likely to be made en route.[10]

Even when the rations arrived, they could present problems of sharing them out in a fair manner:

> Presently our acting QMS [Quartermaster Sergeant] arrived with a sack, which was hauled up into the loft with some difficulty, and proceeded to issue out the rations according to 'messes'. The average number in a 'mess' was four, but some parties drew for two, some for three, others for five; here and there one single man clamoured for his proportion and, in desperation, Hurford brigadied two or three irreconcilables together and treated them as a mess, regardless of their feelings. The difficulty of splitting up cheese, tins of margarine, jam etc., among such varying quantities can be imagined.[11]

He contrasts this somewhat mixed experience with an account of a chance encounter with an army cook. When making his way down a communication trench to join his unit, the young soldier had a very pleasant surprise:

I found to my delight that I had stumbled across a kind of soup kitchen. The Tommy in charge was stirring a copperful of 'Shackles' (soup made from the very dregs of army cooking and stirred with a stick). I must have looked in need of extra nourishment for he said 'D'yer want a drop, son?' 'Yes please,' I replied, 'if you can spare it.' The warmth and zest from that beefy liquid, unexpected as it was, compelled me to accept a second bowlful which I drank with the same enthusiasm as the first.[12]

If food in the frontline could vary, rations for men who were out of the line could be surprisingly generous. Private John Jackson recalled that, at Essars in Flanders, the day's menu consisted of:

Breakfast: chipped potatoes, steak and bacon, fried onions, coffee, bread and butter.
Dinner: roast chicken, boiled potatoes and carrots, rice pudding, coffee and biscuits, wine, cognac, and beer.
Tea: Bacon and eggs, tea, cake and biscuits.
Supper: Coffee, cake, bottled raspberries and cream, followed by a good glass of 'rum punch' as a night-cap.[13]

One surprising element of the experience of being out of the line is illuminated by Private Dolden: 'This was followed by a good feed with knife and fork, implements almost forgotten...'[14] When at the front, a knife and fork was largely dispensed with and replaced by use of a jack knife and spoon. The former item was fastened to the user by a lanyard around the waist or clipped to a belt so it could not be easily lost, and the spoon could be slipped into a pocket or tucked into the top of a man's puttees so it could be located in a hurry. Even today, a so-called 'racing spoon' forms a vital item of kit for soldiers in the modern British Army.

Diet Sheet for week

Meals	Sunday	Monday	Tuesday	Wednesday	Thursday	Friday	Saturday
Battalion Breakfast	Tea Bread Butter Kippers	Tea Bread Butter Bacon	Tea Bread Butter Sausage	Tea Bread Butter Bacon	Tea Bread Butter Fritters	Tea Bread Butter Boiled Bacon	Tea Bread Butter Rissole
Left half Batt Dinner	Roast meat Potatoes Plum pudding & syrup	Irish Stew dumplings Bread Butter Pudding	Roast meat Potatoes Currant Roll	Boil'd Beef carrots Potatoes Barley rice pudding	Roast meat Potatoes Yorkshire pudding	Curried mutton & Rice potatoes Potatoes	Roast Beef Potatoes Yorkshire Pudding
Right half Batt Dinner	Irish Stew dumplings Bread Butter Pudding	Bake meat Potatoes plum pudding syrup	Boil Beef boiled Potato Bohs rice Pudding	Roast mutton Potatoes Currant roll	Curried mutton rice mashed Potato Jam roll	Roast meat Potatoes Yorkshire Pudding	Rissoles rice Potatoes Bread Butter Pudding
Battalion Tea	Bread Butter & Jam	Bread Butter sardines Cake	Bread Butter watercress	Bread Butter Beetroot salad	Bread Butter & Jam	Bread Butter Plain cake	Bread Butter Lettuce
Battalion Supper	Bread Cheese Pickles	Pea Soup	Tomato Soup	Barley Soup	Lentil Soup	Vegetable Soup	Bread & Cold meat

Early tea & Biscuits at 6.30 a.m.

From Log Book of Pte A. Flitney.

More importantly, time out of the trenches, battery position or day-to-day routine, meant the opportunity to supplement issue rations with food and drink bought locally. This could be either from organisations such as the YMCA, Red Cross or Expeditionary Force Canteen (EFC), or from local civilians. The estaminet, the unique cross between bar and café, which sprung up wherever the enterprising French or Belgian could find a surviving building and customers, became a feature of virtually every soldier's experience of the Western Front. The term 'plonk' for cheap wine dates from a period when British soldiers, who preferred white to red wine, ordered glasses of 'vin blanc'. Egg and chips were also an ideal alternative to bully beef and plum and apple jam. Private Beatson comments that, after an exhausting time in the trenches, a meal purchased in a café behind the lines was more than a tonic: 'A good feed and a wash set me on my legs again. The feed nothing elaborate, in a house-café, cost for two; 3Fr [Francs] 20c [Centimes].'[15] On another occasion, he wrote: 'We rose this morning about 8 o'clock after a comfortable night on the straw Watson and I went out to a café and had a tuck in to coffee and buttered rolls'.[16]

At the outbreak of the war in August 1914, the Regular Army's ration strength was 125,000. On mobilisation they were joined by reservists, who expanded this force to over 300,000 men in the course of a few weeks. By November this initial force had been joined by a further 300,000 Territorials. At the same time hundreds of thousands of men rushed to volunteer, virtually swamping the pre-war system of organisation with men who had to be fed, housed and equipped.[17] By the end of the Great War more than 5¼ million men and women were in British uniform and more than 2 million of these were on the Western Front.[18]

One of the oft-quoted facts about the war is that more forage for horses was shipped to the Western Front than ammunition. Some historians have chosen to interpret this as being evidence of cavalry-obsessed British generals. A look at the statistics, however, demonstrates that at its greatest strength, in September 1916, the cavalry represented 2.5 per cent of the manpower of the British Expeditionary Force (BEF). This had dropped to 1.3 per cent in June 1918.[19] So why were so many horses being fed? The answer is the subject of this book. The figures are:

Dead-weight tonnage shipped to France from 9 August 1914 to 10 November 1918	
Ammunition	5,253,338
Food, General	3,240,948
Oats and Hay	5,438,602
Expeditionary Force Canteen	269,517[20]

Even after the expansion of mechanised vehicles, the BEF remained, essentially, a horse-drawn army. Horses were used to move guns, ammunition, pontoons, supplies and both rations and fodder. Even the most ill-used infantryman could not fight a battle every day and even the artillery were not in constant action. However, from August 1914 to 11 November 1918 and beyond, men and women of the BEF expected to be fed every day, and they were. Despite the appalling conditions of trench warfare, transport problems, mud and the weather, the men and women in the forces were fed every day. If the meals they received were not always delicious, they were filling and sustaining. It is no coincidence that the motto of the Army Catering Corps (ACC) was 'We Sustain!' The motto remains that of the modern Royal Logistic Corps (RLC) and this book tells the story of how that miracle of sustenance was achieved.

GLOSSARY OF CULINARY TERMS

ALDERSHOT OVEN: issued by the Army Ordnance Corps (AOC) and made of curved sheets of iron with matching ends which acted as doors. These ovens could be transported easily on wagons, roofed over with earth or clay and used for baking and roasting.

BISCUIT: issued when bread was not available. These durable military biscuits were made from flour with a little fat and salt. They were so hard that they were normally broken up and added to stews or soaked in a liquid to make them edible.

BULLY BEEF OR BULLY: corned beef is beef cooked, preserved and tinned. Chiefly from Argentina. A staple of men in the trenches, they were advised to pierce the tin before fully opening them. If they hissed, they had gone off!

BURGUE OR BURGOO: porridge. Occasionally applied by Australians to stew.

CAMP KETTLE: *see* Dixie.

MESS TIN OR CANTEEN: a tinned steel container and cooking receptacle. Those for the infantry were 'D' shaped and the mounted troops' variation was circular. Each had a lid which could be used as a frying pan or drinking vessel, and a larger bottom element which could be used for cooking more substantial meals. Both variations had a cotton cover to reduce noise and to keep the dirty exterior from fouling uniform or equipment.

CLASP OR 'JACK' KNIFE: issue knife worn attached to a lanyard around the waist or attached to a belt so it could not be easily lost. The knife came with a blade, tin opener and 'marlin' spike for making holes in everything, from an ill-fitting belt to a tin of condensed milk.

COOKER: field kitchen.

CHAR: tea – from the Hindustani *chai*.

DIXIE: a large, oval, tinned steel cooking vessel with a lid and folding metal handle. The word is not from the USA, but from the Indian *degs-chai*, a cooking pot. Also officially called a Camp Kettle.

DUFF: pudding, especially boiled suet pudding. Also a noun − to do a job badly, from the Cockney slang of the 1850s when trading in inferior goods.

DULAY, DUPAN: milk and bread, from the French *du lait* and *du pain*.

EFC: Expeditionary Force Canteens. Run by volunteers from huts erected behind the lines for the sale of groceries, cakes, tobacco etc.

EGG AND CHIPS (French *Oeuf et Frites*): the most popular meal to be served in estaminets. A wartime invention probably due to the high price of meat.

ESTAMINET: On the Western Font an estaminet was a combination of pub, café and restaurant. Found in villages and small towns, it was universally run by a proprietress who was assisted by younger female staff. A place of rest and relaxation for men away from the front, the estaminet was the subject of much ribald comment and some optimistic speculation relating to those that ran them.

FRIGO: frozen or chilled meat. A French slang word for *viande frigorifee*.

***GRAND BON OEUF AND FRITES*:** a soldier's term for egg and chips.

GUN FIRE: Tea served to troops before the first parade of the day, sometimes with the addition of rum. The derivation may be the original 'gunpowder' or fine green tea, which had become applied to common tea in the mid-nineteenth century.

HAVERSACK: small pack used to carry rations and small necessaries. The origin appears to relate to oat 'havercakes' from the original Norse and later Yorkshire slang. The 33rd Foot (First Yorkshire West Riding) were later known as the 'Havercake Boys'.

HAY BOX: a container of wood or metal in which hot food was carried surrounded and insulated by hay. This kept the food warm and extended the cooking period.

IRON RATIONS: a supply of rations, sufficient for one day, carried by soldiers in action. They were packed in tins, hence 'Iron Ration'.

JAPAN: bread, from the French *du pain*. Some suggest that this word was introduced by the New Army troops, replacing the older and Regular Army term, Rooty.

JIPPO: juice or gravy, especially bacon fat. Sometimes stew.

KFS: knife, fork and spoon: These issue items were usually marked with the owner's regimental number to prevent loss. In the trenches the knife and fork were dispensed with and many soldiers kept a 'racing spoon' tucked into their puttees, ready for a quick start to a meal.

MACONOCHIE: a tinned ration of meat and vegetables, usually pork and beans, named after the company that manufactured the product in Aberdeen. Not universally popular, with at least one man suggesting that the product was a war crime.

PLUM AND APPLE: *see* Pozzy and Tickler's.

POINT BLANK: white wine, from the French *vin blanc*.

POMFRITZ: chips (potato), from the French *pommes de terres frites*.

PLONK, OR OCCASIONALLY BLONK: wine, usually white and cheap, from the French *vin blanc*.

POZZY OR POSSY: jam, probably from the issue of condensed milk of the Posy Brand early in the war. This was used as substitute for jam on bread and the term remained, even when jam was available.

POZZY-WALLAH: a man keen on jam.

***QUART SOU* OR FOUR SOU, LOW DENOMINATION COINS, IN ENGLISH:** the price of a glass of cheap wine, usually red, which became a term for wine in general.

ROOTY: bread, from the Urdu word *roti*. The term originated with units in India and was brought with them to the Western Front.

ROOTY MEDAL: Long Service Medal earned by eating army rations for a long period.

SKILLY: thin stew. Also a civilian term for soup in workhouses.

SOYER STOVE: the standard form of cooker in the British Army from the 1850s until after the Falklands War in 1982. Designed by Alexis Soyer for use in the Crimean War, it consisted of a 12 gallon (gal) (55 litre (l)) boiler inside an iron cylinder with a chimney and fireplace. It used any form of solid fuel, was highly efficient and did not show flames, which might betray the position of a field kitchen.

SMOKE: any form of cigarette or pipe tobacco.

SPOTTED DOG OR SPOTTED DICK: currant pudding.

SRD: Service Ration Depot. The initials marked on the body of a jar or container which may contain rum, but also lime juice or other ration liquids. Not 'Service Rum Dilute' or 'Seldom Reaches Destination' as Tommies guessed it to mean.

TEA BUCKET: a simple tinned steel bucket provided with a spout and lid in which 3gal (13½l) of tea could be carried.

TOASTING FORK: A bayonet, which was often used for this purpose rather than as a weapon.

TICKLER'S: the name of the manufacturer of the standard jam, plum and apple, issued early in the war. Tickler's then became the generic term for all types of jam. The tins were also used to provide the containers for early improvised grenades – Tommy Tickler's Artillery.

TOMMY: bread. An older term than Rooty or Japan.

TOMMY COOKER: a tin, solid fuel stove, either privately purchased or issued when no other method of cooking was available.

TOT: the issue of rum ½ gill (71 millilitres (ml)): sixty-four tots to the gallon.

TOT SACK: a bag for carrying rations, usually a sandbag.

WADS: cakes or buns sold in the Dry (no alcohol) Canteen: Hence Wad, Scoffer or Wad Puncher for a teetotaller. 'Wads' could also be used to indicate sandwiches.

INTRODUCTION

From 1815 to 1914

THE DUKE OF Wellington's preparation for the campaign in the Peninsula included the development of a working commissariat (department of the army charged with providing food and forage), but this does not mean that this was easy or that the treasury in Whitehall were happy with the additional expense. One problem was that, on the outset of the operations, the commissaries were mostly inexperienced and they had a skeleton staff to superintend the supplies to all units. At this time, rations were issued by the commissariat in the evening, usually for three days at a time. One day's ration was issued to the men, while the others were held at a regimental headquarters. In Spain in 1813, every soldier was entitled to a daily ration of a 1 pound (lb) of meat, 1lb of biscuit (or 1½lb of bread), and a quart of beer (or a pint of wine, or a ⅓ pint of spirits). When the army halted, ovens were built so that bread could be baked and meat was obtained from butchered cattle, which had been driven along behind the marching columns. The meat was usually boiled by small messes of soldiers in a communal pot, to which was added pulses and vegetables. This provided a soup for the evening and a joint of cooked meat, which could be eaten cold the next day. It was during the Peninsula War that British soldiers were first issued with an individual cooking vessel called, not surprisingly, the 'mess tin'. This was a two-part, tin-plated steel item, roughly D-shaped, to fit against the body or pack, and provided with a handle so it could be held over a fire or used as an eating vessel. It was far from ideal, as too much heat would cause the tin plate to melt and soldiers cooking for themselves used vastly more fuel than communal cookery.

However, the ability to make tea and, in some cases coffee, was recognised as a valuable contribution to the soldier's diet.

ARMY COOK'S TIP NO.1

To discover whether coffee is pure, sprinkle a few grains on the surface of a tumberful of water. If pure, they will float but if adulterated they will sink to the bottom.

From Log Book of GNR Smith, 368 Siege Battery, RGA, May 1917

In the period after the Battle of Waterloo in 1815, greater importance had been attached to feeding the army, and the construction of barracks throughout the country meant that it was easy to superintend the feeding of troops. Previously they had been quartered on willing civilians or in public houses, where they were supplied by the residents at the government's expense. At the beginning of the nineteenth century the soldier's ration at home comprised 1lb of bread and ¾lb of meat daily – for this food 6*d* per day was stopped from his pay – and, although cooking facilities were available in the new barracks, they were of a very basic character. The cooking utensils available to each company were two copper pots ('coppers'), one for potatoes and the other for meat, which were always boiled, as no ovens were available for roasting or baking, and so the soldier had to put up with the eternal boiled beef and beef broth served as hot or cold meat for his two meals per day. Breakfast was served at 7.30 a.m. and dinner at 12.30 p.m., after which he was without food unless he was able to purchase something to sustain him for the next nineteen hours.[21] Although this might seem surprising to modern diners, it was clearly perfectly acceptable at the time and an order for the army issued by the Adjutant General's Office, dated 1 January 1882, makes it clear that the system was carefully regulated:

In Camp or Barracks the Captain or Subaltern of the Day must visit and inspect the Kettles at the hour appointed for Cooking, and no Kettle is to be taken from the Kitchens till this inspection is made, and the Signal is given for the Men to dine, which should be at the same hour throughout the Garrison or Camp. Independent of this Regimental Arrangement, the Officers must daily and hourly attend to the Messing, and to every circumstance connected with the Economy of their Troops and Companies.[22]

In the period of peace that followed the end of the Napoleonic Wars there were few occasions when the Home Army had the opportunity for collective training, and in 1853 a 'camp of exercise' was established on Cobham Common, under the direction of the Prince Consort and the Duke of Cambridge. This two-month exercise was designed to give every regiment of cavalry and infantry, together with the artillery, engineers and all supporting services, the opportunity to co-operate as a force under active service conditions. Wells had already been sunk to supply fresh water, and the kitchens were specially built from mud over the trenches. Although the results of the experiment were not conclusive, they were a useful preparation for the force that would be sent to the Crimea just two years later. Although the invasion of the Crimea and the Battle of the Alma were successful, the Siege of Sebastopol, which began in the autumn of 1854, was to be a disaster. The principal reason for the high death rate at Sebastopol was not enemy action, but the inability of the army to supply the soldiers in the trenches overlooking the city with food, fuel or safe water. This situation has commonly been ascribed to the army's neglect of supply in the preceding period of peace. It was, in fact, the result of treasury penny-pinching, such as the abolition of the Royal Wagon Train in 1833, which had been established in the Peninsula War to assist the commissariat. The intention was that, in peacetime, the wagon train had no function and could be axed. It was planned, at least by the treasury, that local wagons and horses would be hired in any future campaign. These were not forthcoming when the 'Army of the East' landed on Russian soil and supply handicapped the first year of the war until the innovative solution of a specially constructed military railway provided a 'modern' form of transport.

Another innovation of the campaign was the arrival of Alexis Soyer, who was born in France but by 1837 had become head chef at the Reform Club in London, and who later became an expert on economical charity cookery[23]. Soyer took with him the first prototypes of his famous field-cooking stove: this was cylindrical and it stood on short legs, under the lid was a copper and below was the fire, fed through a small hatch in the front centre, the cowled chimney rising up from the back. The inventor had refused to patent it in case anyone would think that his offer of the 'Soyer Stove' to the army had been made for his personal profit.[24] The stove took his name and would continue to be used by the British Army on campaigns as varied as the Zulu War, the First and Second World Wars, the Falklands War and, finally, the First Gulf War in 1991. The great advantages of the Soyer Stove were the economical way in which it used fuel, it was light and portable and could be used without the flame being seen. As the stove could be used for stews, roasting, baking and steaming, plus making tea, coffee and hot chocolate, its adaptability was a great asset and an enormous advantage over previous systems of open fire cookery. Soyer started work in the hospitals at Scutari, where he revised the diets of the staff and patients and introduced new catering procedures, so that instead of the so-called cooking of the basic rations of 1lb meat, bread and potatoes, he drew up numerous menus of soups, stews and seasoned meat, and supplemented the diet by local purchases and introduced beef tea, jellies and rice for the invalid diet.

From Log Book of Pte C. Leveratt, 1916.

Beef Tea Recipe

- Cut meat into small pieces, remove all fat and skin.
- Place into cooking vessel, add cold water.
- Allow to stew gently till [sic] all strength is extracted, removing scum as it rises on top.
- A good method is to place the beef in jar with lid & required amount of water & place in oven.
- Strain through fine seive [*sic*] or muslin about 1 quart of cold water to 1lb of beef.

From Log Book of Pte C. Leveratt, No. 32880, E Company,
1st Garr. Battn, Worcester Regt, 1916

In late August 1855, Soyer officially opened his first camp and bivouac kitchen at Sebastopol and, using seven large Soyer Stoves, a banquet was prepared entirely from army rations. His rations were distributed and a succession of army cooks were introduced to the new system. This was a necessary development as the Commission of Enquiry held in 1857 into the sanitary state of the army reported: 'The first step must be to instruct our soldiers in the rudiments of the art of cooking, of which they are now lamentably deficient'.[25]

Horace Wyndham, who enlisted in 1890, made this observation concerning the period:

> During the last six years especially barrack feeding has made brilliant strides. Dishes of meat are supplied for breakfast; roast, stews, curries, puddings and pies for dinner; and even the despised tea meal is generally supplemented by some appetising repasts have been replaced not only by an abundance, but by such variety of savoury food that the soldier who still complains of hunger must be either a fool or a glutton.[26]

By contrast, he singles out some of the men taken into regimental cookhouses who were without the slightest aptitude for the work: 'They were haphazardly taken from the ranks, and pitch-forked in a kitchen.'[27]

SCHEDULE III.

SPECIMEN OF A BATTERY, SQUADRON, OR COMPANY DIET SHEET.

MEALS.	SUNDAY.	MONDAY.	TUESDAY.	WEDNESDAY.	THURSDAY.	FRIDAY.	SATURDAY.	REMARKS.
Breakfast...	Tea, Coffee, or Cocoa, Fried Bacon.	Tea, Coffee, or Cocoa, Butter.	Tea, Coffee, or Cocoa, Haddocks.	Tea, Coffee, or Cocoa, Butter.	Tea, Coffee, or Cocoa, Sausages and Mashed Potatoes.	Tea, Coffee, or Cocoa, Butter.	Tea, Coffee, or Cocoa, Boiled Bacon (Cold).	
Dinner ...	Baked Meat, with Potatoes and Apple Tarts.	Irish Stew. and Rice Pudding.	Roast Meat, Stuffed, and Pea Soup.	Meat Pies and Cabbage.	Roast Meat. Potatoes and Plum Pudding.	Turkish Pillau and Cabbage.	Tomato Soup, Roast Meat, Yorkshire Pudding, Potatoes.	
Tea ...	Tea, Bread and Butter.	Tea and Marmalade	Tea, Butter, and Salad.	Tea, Butter, and Cheese.	Tea, Butter.	Tea and Dripping.	Tea and Butter.	

Things to note when compiling a weekly Diet Sheet.

1. The diet must be good and varied, no dish to be served twice during the week.
2. No two dishes containing the same ingredients should be served at one meal, *e.g.*, Pea or Lentil Soup, and Haricot Beans or Peas. Meat Pies and a pudding made of flour, Rice with Curry and Tapioca, Rice or Sago Pudding.
3. Green and other vegetables should be given in fair proportion ; also Salads when in season.
4. The diet should be so arranged that the men may have a roasting joint one day and a stewing joint next, and so on.
5. Following points must be considered :—Price of materials, the money to be expended, the tastes of the men, and the times when fish, &c., are in season, as these are sometimes cheaper when plentiful.

From 'Manual of Military Cooking, 1910'.

Wyndham also remained unconvinced that the catering was well organised and commented on overcrowded cookhouses, badly cooked meat and the delay between food being prepared for inspection and service. If food in barracks was often poor, preparing hot meals for troops in the field was dealt with by a combination of Soyer Stoves, improvised ovens using trenches and constructions of clay, turf or even hollowed out anthills, as well as the 'Aldershot Oven' (more of which later). During the campaign in South Africa, 1899–1902, mention is frequently made of corned beef (bully beef) and a 'Maconochie' ration, an innovation of meat and vegetables. These could be eaten from the tin or added to the 'camp kettles' or 'dixies' to produce an all-in-one stew. These tinned rations would form a staple for the war that followed.

SCHEDULE II.
FIELD COOKING.

Being the Diet of three Companies of Mounted Infantry encamped at Bourley, near Aldershot, for the week ending 5th Sept., 1891.

Specimen of Military Diet in a Standing Camp for One Week.

GOVERNMENT RATIONS.

Meat, 16 ozs., including bone } Net value, 6¾d.
Bread, 16 ozs.

MESSING MONEY.

3d. per diem deducted from daily pay of each Soldier.

Total nett cost per man, per diem, including fuel ... ... 9¾d.

APPARATUS AND FUEL.

Broad Arrow Kitchen.	Service Kettle, 12 quarts.
Aldershot Oven.	" 7 "
Soyer's Stoves for Stock.	3lbs. of wood per man per diem.

NOTES.

The Dripping saved during the month of July, 1891, was 9,536 ozs. or 596 lbs., valued at £9 18s. 0d., being at the rate of £115 per annum for 874 men.

One lb. of meat and bone produced nearly 1 oz. of Dripping in addition to Stock.

A tent or shelter for cooks must be provided.

REMARKS.

The extra ¼ lb. of meat allowed for troops under canvas is used to provide a meat breakfast. Alternate companies or half-companies.

The staff of cooks required are—1 Serjeant-Cook, 1 assistant to keep Stock and Dripping (with returns), and 1 cook and 1 assistant per company.

MILITARY FIELD DIET.

Under the new system of cooking.

Nos. V., IX., and X. COMPANIES, MOUNTED INFANTRY.

REGIMENTAL FIELD DIET RETURN.

SCALE OF DIET FOR WEEK ENDING 5TH SEPTEMBER, 1891.

Troop, Battery, or Company.	Approximate No in Mess.	MEALS.	SUNDAY.	MONDAY.	TUESDAY.	WEDNESDAY.	THURSDAY.	FRIDAY.	SATURDAY.
No. V.	130	Bfst. ⅓Co. ⅔Co. "	Coffee, Bacon, and Steaks.	Coffee, Steaks, and Bacon.	Coffee, Liver and Bacon, and Steaks.	Coffee, Steaks, Liver and Bacon.	Coffee, Liver and Bacon, and Steaks.	Coffee, Eggs and Bacon. Liver-Bacon and Steaks.	Coffee, Liver, Bacon, Steaks—and Eggs and Bacon.
		Dinner	Baked Meat and Potatoes. Plum Pudding.	Brown Curry. Rice and Potatoes.	Roast Meat, Potatoes and Yorkshire Pudding.	Meat Pies and Potatoes.	Baked Meat. Potatoes and Pea Soup.	Curried Stew and Potatoes.	Roast Meat (Stuffed), Potatoes and Barley Soup.
		Tea ...	Tea and Dripping.	Tea and Marmalade.	Tea and Dripping.	Tea and Dripping.	Tea and Jam.	Tea and Dripping.	Tea and Fried Fish.
No. IX.	124	Bfst. ⅓Co. ⅔Co. "	Coffee, Bacon, and Stews.	Coffee, Roast Meat, and Salmon.	Coffee, Liver, Stew, and Beef.	Coffee, Bacon, and Roast Meat.	Coffee, Curried Liver, and Stew.	Coffee, Roast Meat, and Brawn.	Coffee, Stew, and Bacon.
		Dinner	Baked Meat and Stews. Baked Meat and Potatoes. Plum Pudding.	Meat Puddings and Potatoes.	Baked Meat and Potatoes. Plain Suet Pudding.	Baked Meat, Haricot Beans and Potatoes.	Roast Meat, Yorkshire Pudding and Potatoes.	Baked Meat and Potatoes. Plum Pudding.	Sea Pies.
		Tea ...	Tea and Dripping.	Tea and Jam.	Tea and Dripping.	Tea and Fresh Fish.	Tea and Dripping.	Tea and Kippers.	Tea and Syrup.
No. X.	120	Bfst. ⅓Co. ⅔Co. "	Coffee, Bacon, and Beef.	Coffee, Beef, and Brawn.	Coffee, Brawn, and Beef.	Coffee, Beef, and Butter.	Coffee, Butter and Beef.	Coffee, Beef, and Fried Liver.	Coffee, Fried Liver, and Beef.
		Dinner	Baked Meat and Potatoes. Jam Rolls.	Irish Stew.	Roast Meat, Yorkshire Pudding and Potatoes.	Brown Curry. Rice and Potatoes.	Baked Meat, Haricot Beans and Potatoes.	Brown Stew. Currant Potatoes. Rolls.	Baked Meat, Potatoes and Pea Soup.
		Tea ...	Tea and Dripping.	Tea and Marmalade.	Tea and Dripping.	Tea and Fried Fresh Fish.	Tea and Cheese.	Tea and Dripping.	Tea and Dripping.

Bourley Camp, Aldershot.—Date, 20th August, 1891.
(3563)

RAYMOND PORTAL, Capt. & Adjt., Mounted Infantry.

From 'Manual of Military Cooking, 1910'.

On 3 August 1914, with Britain at war with Imperial Germany, the BEF mobilised in support of France and to honour her treaty to preserve Belgium's neutrality. The BEF was sent overseas for what was envisaged as a short war. According to the Kaiser it would be over 'before the leaves fell from the trees', and most thought that it would be 'over by Christmas'. The guns fell silent four years and three months later, on 11 November 1918. By the time of the Armistice that ended the conflict, the ration strength of the British Army was 5,363,352 men and women, and 895,700 animals worldwide. The figure for the BEF in France and Belgium alone was 2,360,400 and 404,000 animals.[28] Despite the appalling conditions of a world conflict – enemy action, transport problems, which included submarine attack, mud and the weather – these men and women were fed every day. To achieve this the ASC had expanded to a strength of 12,000 officers and 320,000 men.[29] This was roughly twice the size of the entire British Army sent to the Continent in 1914.

In early twenty-first-century Britain, the subject of diet and nutrition is focused on the current problems of over-eating and obesity; this was not a problem that faced most members of the population 100 years ago. During the Second Anglo-Boer War, 1899–1902, Britain was forced to expand the army and a large number of volunteers were required. However, it was found that almost half the men who attempted to enlist for the army were physically unfit for military service. Height, lack of chest expansion and disease, resulting from poor nutrition and housing, were all identified as factors. In response to a report from the Director General of the Army Medical Services, a Select Committee on Physical Deterioration was established to examine the situation, and their findings were published in 1904:

The one subject which causes anxiety for the future as regards recruiting is the gradual deterioration of the physique of the working classes from which the bulk of recruits must always be drawn. When it is remembered that recruiters are instructed not to submit men for medical examination unless they are reasonably expected to be passed fit, we cannot but be struck by the percentage considered unfit for service. The poor physical condition of the urban poor is easy to understand when we reflect that their poverty includes defective housing, overcrowding and insanitary conditions.[30]

This convinced the government that some assistance had to be provided to improve the diet and physical condition of the working population, otherwise Britain might be left undefended in the event of a major war. The committee had concluded that, as at least a third of children were malnourished, tuition was required for the working classes in the 'preparation of food and feeding of young children'. The outcome of this was that the first free school meals were provided from 1906 and examination of school children's health began in 1907. However, by the outbreak of war, in 1914, only 158,000 children were being given a free meal once a day at school. It can be concluded that this made a small contribution to off-setting the problem of poor nutrition for the majority of children and that many adults were badly and inadequately fed. In these circumstances it should be of no surprise that many volunteers were rejected because they failed the medical examination at recruiting offices, or that the minimum height for volunteers fell as the war progressed, reflecting the poor physical condition of the population as a whole. It is also worth noting the observation made by many observers, that young volunteers rapidly put on weight and grew in response to the regular meals provided by the army.

ARMY COOK'S TIP NO.2

When cooking apples, add a pinch of salt. This makes them tender and improves the flavour.

From Log Book of G.N.R. Smith, 368 Siege Battery, RGA

One additional reason for the relative good health and physique of soldiers may not simply be related to diet. Although we are familiar with the amount of hard work required for military training and the physical effort required for digging trenches or going into battle, the pattern of labour for the working classes before and during the Great War is daunting. In a world with little mechanization most factory workers were expected to be there for twelve hours a day, six days a week. Mine workers had twelve-hour shifts and farm labourers worked from

6.30 a.m. until 6 p.m. in summer and until dark in winter. Men working with horses on farms did so from 5.30 a.m. and did half an hour's extra work at night to ensure that the animals were fed and groomed.[31] If training for military service was grueling, in contrast to civilian life it may not have been as extreme as we imagine today.

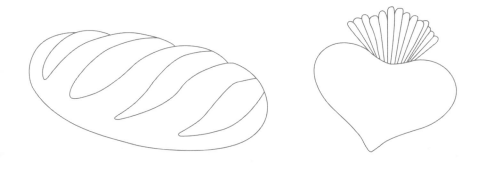

PART ONE

PROFILE OF AN ARMY COOK

IT IS VERY difficult to say what type of soldier was likely to become a cook in the army. There was no official Army Catering Corps until 1941, although from 1870 it was dictated that 'one sergeant cook is to be appointed to every regiment of cavalry, battalion of infantry ... brigade of artillery or command of engineers or military train ...'.[32]

Training was often haphazard and the cooks selected were all too often soldiers that NCOs wanted to remove from the ranks because they were unskilled or difficult. This situation was made worse if the soldier lacked interest or aptitude in his new trade, as many of them did. From 1889, the Queen's Regulations and Orders stated that non-commissioned officers could not hold the appointment of cook without undergoing a course of training at the 'Instructional Kitchen at Aldershot'. The Adjutant-General stated that the candidate should fulfil certain conditions, which included being 'steady and trustworthy' to 'write with accuracy and quickness', and that they should have 'five years to serve'. His duties, as laid out in the Queen's Regulations, include 'personally superintending all cooking done in Regimental Cookhouses', 'to instruct those under him in all operations connected with cookery' and 'he will enforce order, punctuality and cleanliness'.[33] The result was great improvement in the standard of rations and by 1896, the first Army Cookery Competition was held at Aldershot. At the time, Britain's volunteer army was tiny by comparison with her European allies and potential enemies with their vast conscript armies. What could be achieved by the peacetime British Imperial Police Force would be challenged by any rapid expansion of the army.

A CULINARY TEST AS TAKEN BY PTE A.E. PURSSELL,
NO. 39246, 13TH BEDFORDS BATT., NO 1 SECTION, EASTERN COMMAND, SCHOOL OF COOKERY, PRITSLADE, SUSSEX, 1917

Ques: What does the modified field ration consist of?
Ans:
14oz of bread
12oz of meat
2oz of sugar
2oz of bacon
½oz tea
¼oz salt

5½ in cash per man per day
10½oz of flour can be drawn down in lieu of bread

Ques: How does a cook obtain his pay?
Ans:
By the sale of by products (not including swill)
11)- realised for 100 men in mess entitles a cook to obtain 6d per day
9)- realised entitles him to 3d per day
Less than 9/- he gets nothing

Ques: When do you get bacon?
Ans: Every other morning

Ques: How much dripping should each ration produce?
Ans: A least ½oz

Ques: What are by products used for?
Ans:

| 1st Class dripping | Pastry |
| | Issues in lieu of margarine |

All other dripping is sold for the extraction of glycerines, which is turned into nitroglycerine for high explosive shells

| Bones | |
| Sweated Stuff | For agricultural purposes |

Ques: How much meat is saved daily in each ration?
Ans: About 2oz which provide rissoles, sausages, etc for breakfast

Ques: What are the chief duties of a cook?
Ans: Cleanliness, Economy, Punctuality, Simmer, Skim, Scour, System

Ques: What number are the following regulated to cook for?
Ans:

Travelling Cooker	252 men
Aldershot Oven	220 men
Soyer Stove	50 men (make tea for about 90)
Camp Kettle	15 without vegetables
	8 with vegetables

Ques: Give the ingredients for scones for 30 men?
Ans:

1½lb flour	
¾lb breadcrumbs	¾oz of farta (?)
6oz dripping	¾oz carbonated soda
6oz sugar	

Ques: How much water & tea is required to make tea for 100 men?
Ans: 13 gallons of water, 1lb of tea
Ques: What is dripping?
Ans: Dripping is the oil extracted from the ration during the process of cooking it can be classed under 2 heads namely first & second class it is used for

1) Pastes [pastry]
2) Puddings
3) Issued in lieu of margarine (breakfast, tea)
4) Frying purposes

Ques: What amount is required for 100 men of the following:
Ans:

Roast meat	70lb	10oz per man
Baked meat	70lb	10oz per man
All other dinners	60lb	9oz per man
Sausages & Rissoles	21lb	4oz per man
Steaks	25lb	4oz per man
Mutton Chops	31¼lb	5oz per man

[Sadly, we do not know how Pte Purssell scored in this test!]

Only three years later, the war against the Boers in South Africa plunged Britain and the Empire into a three-year conflict, during which an army of half a million men was deployed. These vast expansions in the size of the forces proved a mammoth task in terms of catering, especially as so many of the new cooks detailed from the ranks were untrained. However, no major reform took place between the end of the Anglo-Boer War in 1902 and the outbreak of the First World War in August 1914. Cooks remained regimental soldiers who were trained in peacetime by the Army Service Corps at the Army Cookery School at Aldershot. In wartime this became somewhat more ad hoc, and although numerous cookery schools were established during the war, and an Inspector of Catering appointed in 1914, not all cooks had the opportunity to attend a course. The Army Catering Corps was not established until 1941 and, until then, there was no centralised system of army cooks. In 1916, on the Somme, Private Dolden of the London Scottish reported that:

> One of the Company cooks was sent to a neighbouring village to cook for a party of Scottish who were there on a bombing course. Lance Corporal Arnot, who was in charge of 'D' Company cooker, asked me therefore, if I would temporarily fill the vacancy … I had not the faintest idea about cooking, but ignorance seemed to be the only qualification for a job in the army.[34]

His training was 'on the job', although he clearly benefitted, as did the soldiers he fed, from enthusiasm and professional pride combined with hard work.

MANUAL OF MILITARY COOKING AND DIETARY, 1918
DUTIES OF SERJEANT-COOK AND COOKS

The serjeant-cook will have complete control over the cooks of his regiment or battalion, who should receive their orders from him.

He will detail each cook to the apparatus suitable for preparing the various dishes required for the following day, dividing the work so that each man may know what he has to do, in addition to the cooking.

He will afford every facility for varying the diet of the several messes, so that each may have a complete change daily throughout the week; and will arrange that the messes using the oven one day shall have use of the boilers the next day, and so on.

He will be personally responsible that no misappropriation of any kind whatever takes place, and should be present when the milk is issued with a list of quantities ordered, to ensure that each mess receives the correct amount.

Groceries should be received by the serjeant-cook, who will weigh each day the quantities of the various articles received for each mess, and satisfy himself that they agree with the diet sheet and are the correct quantities for the number of men in mess. He will lock them up and retain the key. He will issue the various articles to each cook, and will see that the full quantity as issued is actually used, and that it is prepared by the cooks according to the instructions given.

When imparting instructions, the serjeant cook should illustrate his meaning by taking any particular dish and preparing it himself, giving full details during its preparation. When at some future time the same dish is being prepared, he will see that his previous instructions are carried out, checking errors on the part of the cook. Patience and tact are required, especially with young soldiers, in training them in their duties as cooks.

Assistant cooks should be trained by the serjeant-cook with a view to replacing the cooks when required.

> The meat when issued to the cook will be placed in the dish belonging to the particular mess for which it is intended, care being taken to mark the dish with the number of the mess.
>
> When nets are used for vegetables, &c., a tablet or piece of wood, with the number of each mess plainly marked thereon, should be attached to each.
>
> Cooks should not be allowed to have their meals in the cookhouse. Smoking is not permitted in the kitchens.

From 'Manual of Military Cooking and Dietary, 1918'.

Another cook had a more conventional form of training: Christopher Leveratt registered for the Derby scheme as a potential recruit on 10 December 1915 and he was called up in June of the following year.[35] At the time he was 29 years old, a married man with three children living in South Hampstead, London and a trained butcher. Despite his place of residence, he was posted to the Worcestershire Regiment. This was a common occurrence by 1916, by which time casualties and variation in the numbers of men coming forward as volunteers meant that the War Office simply assigned recruits to units, regardless of their location. Between 3 August and 12 September 1916, he attended a cooking course for army cooks at Weymouth. We can presume his selection for the course was due to his trade as butcher. This thirty-nine-day course appears to have been very thorough. Private Leveratt's Log Book gives a breakdown of a Company cook's day. This begins at 5.30 a.m. with reveille (well before the other men were woken), followed by lighting fires at 6 a.m. and breakfast at 7 a.m. What follows is a programme of daily activity that details what should be happening in the kitchen every hour of the day. Such a regimen would have applied in theory to all army cooks.

THE COOK'S DAY

5.30	Light fires for Breakfast and open windows.
6.00	Prepare meat for any Puddings, Pies or Stews.
7.00	Cook Breakfast, prepare coffee or tea.
7.30	Light fires required for dinner, make coffee or tea.
7.45	Send up breakfast and close cookhouse during breakfast.
8.30	Prepare dinner and give practical instruction for assistant cooks.
9.30	Inspect stock pot and see that bones are small.
10.00	Make dripping and label 1st and 2nd class.
10.30	Inspect cookhouse and see that everything is clean.
11.00	Inspect dinners and point out any mistakes.
11.30	Place on potatoes etc for dinner.
12.00	Carving to be commenced if Roast or Baked meat.
12.30	Dinners to be laid out in the respective messes for inspection.
12.40	Send up dinners, fill up boilers and draw fires not required.
2.00	Sergt Cooks take over groceries etc, check them, hands over required ingredients to cooks and locks up remainder.
2.15	Prepare next days food as far as possible, sausages, etc
3.30	Make soup for evening and prepare for tea.
4.30	Make tea.
4.45	Serve tea, lay fires for next morning. First thoroughly cleaning the apparatus and lock up the cookhouse for the day.
Note	Fat to be skimmed from all stews, stock pot etc, during the process of cooking.

The above is a rough idea of the duties for the cooks that must be verified [varied] according to conditions prevailing in the battalion.

From Log Book of Cpl P.R. Froud, Feb. 1917

Even with a large team of cooks, the Camp Kitchen was not a place to take it easy and although the cooks would have avoided at least some duties, such as guards, they would be expected to be fighting soldiers. There are frequent accounts of units in extreme circumstances calling upon the cooks and drivers to put up a defence; this would require weapons training and one wonders how they managed to fit this in. It may, however, have been a welcome change from the endless round of preparation, cooking and cleaning called for in the cookhouse.

MANUAL OF MILITARY COOKING AND DIETARY, 1918
KITCHENS

Everything connected with the kitchen should be scrupulously clean.

The walls of the kitchen will be swept in the early morning before they become damp from steam.

The windows will be cleaned at least once a week; during the day they will be kept open at the top, to ventilate the kitchen and to allow steam to escape.

A few pages later in Leveratt's Log Book, the kitchen rules would be familiar to any modern budding chef. Smoking is strictly forbidden, taps should not be 'unattended when turned on' and there should be 'no sitting down or lounging on tables'. No 'taking any food except for tasting purposes' and it was not permitted to leave the 'kitchen without permission'. The last item on the list sounds very familiar: a cook must not leave the 'Sink Dirty'.[36]

Cooks were expected to be familiar with the various types of ingredients they would be presented with, and as part of their training they learned the various portions of animals, so they could detect sub-standard meat and, potentially, act as butchers. The 'Notes With Regard To Meat Inspection' is a background for cooks and makes it clear that live, dead and frozen meat may be provided and the cook must be ready to inspect and approve each category.[37]

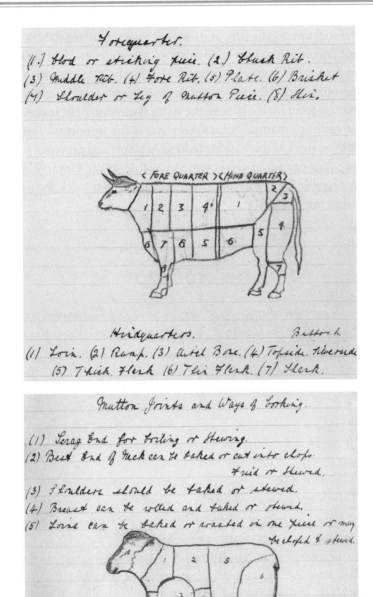

Forequarters.

(1.) blod or striking puie. (2.) blush Rib.
(3) Middle Rib. (4) Fore Rib. (5) Plate. (6) Brisket
(7) Shoulder or Leg of Mutton Puie. (8) Shin.

Hindquarters.   Buttock

(1) Loin. (2) Rump. (3) Aitch Bone. (4) Topside, silverside
(5) Thick Flank (6) Thin Flank. (7) Shank.

Mutton Joints and Ways of Cooking.

(1) Scrag End for boiling or stewing.
(2) Best End of Neck can be baked or cut into chops.
                                    Fried or stewed.
(3) Shoulders should be baked or stewed.
(4) Breast can be rolled and baked or stewed.
(5) Loins can be baked or roasted in one puie or may
                                    be chofed & stewed.

(6) Legs may be roasted baked or boiled.

From Log Book of Cpl P.R. Froud, 1917.

The manual covers the preparation and cooking of vegetables in a few pages, but encourages cooks to add nettles, sweet docks, wild mushrooms and even marigold flowers to dishes.[38] This might come as a surprise, but when one considers the various situations an army cook might find himself preparing food in, looking to the natural environment makes sense.

All the military manuals of cookery stress the importance of a good 'Stock Pot', as stock is the base ingredient of soups and gravies.[39] Although Oxo and other prepared cubes were available in the Great War, it was clearly preferable for the cooks to prepare their own stock from the left-over food in the kitchen.

THE STOCK POT

A stock pot should be established in every barracks and field kitchen to provide good stock which forms the basis of all soups, gravies, sauces, etc. it consists of a large boiler or a large cooking utensil, into which should be placed all available bones etc. To start the stock pot it should be 3 parts full of water then collect all bones that are cut from the ration meat, chop them up small and place in the boiler and allow to simmer gently from 6 to 8 hours. They should be allowed to simmer longer if possible, so as to obtain all the nutriment possible from them. Skim off any fat as it appears on the surface. The bones should be taken out every night and placed into bags and sold. The stock should be poured into a clean vessel, and the stock pot thoroughly cleaned out and turned upside down to air.

The next day fresh bones should be used and the stock remaining from the previous day poured back into the stock pot, with fresh water added as required and carried on in this manner from day to day.

In small units where the bones are small in quantity they may be kept for 3 days, but should be distinctly marked so that at the end of the third day they may be placed in sacks and sold. They should be removed from the stock each night, and hung in a dry, cool place. Every effort should be made in cookhouses to reserve a special vessel for keeping stock, in order that the surplus portion of the unused stock may be put away from day to day. This process adds considerably to the stock made.

From Log Book of Cpl P.R. Froud, Feb. 1917

In the days before the modern problems with animal food being contaminated with human food waste, cooks were responsible for the recovery of 'swill'. The 'Swill Tub' contained all waste food and all vegetable cuttings and scrapings. The contents of the tub were sold to farmers and the money credited to the mess account.[40] One wartime source indicates that a monthly contract with a farmer, based on a mess of 100 men, should produce 10s (50p).[41] To put this in context, a private soldier earned 1s (5p) per day. Another source of income was 'dripping' (oil and fat) recovered from cooking. Some was used for future food preparation but the bulk could be clarified and sold. There were two classes of dripping, the best being from meat suet and the other from roasting and the preparation of stock.[42]

SWILL TUB

The swill tub is a receptacle for all waste food stuffs collected after meals and all cuttings of vegetables in preparation. It should be placed as far from the kitchen as circumstance will admit and will thereby assure freedom from smells and in the presence of flies kept down. it should be at least 60 yards from cookhouse.

Indications
A study of the swill tub will be found to show the following
1st If an excess of food has been prepared the swill tubs will be full.
2nd Whether the men are tired of any one dish.
3rd If food is badly cooked.

BY PRODUCTS
DRIPPING BONES, CRACKLING, ETC

These things are used for making high explosives or soap or many other things useful for the progress of War:

Dripping Bones are worth   48 per ton

Bones   6 per ton

Dry bones and marrow   7 per ton

Crackling if pressed   3 10s per ton

Crackling if not pressed   9 10s per ton

One man's ration of meat, cook should save 1oz dripping per day and not less than ½oz a cook.

MEN'S MESSING.

DRIPPING RECOVERIES AND BY-PRODUCTS DIARY.

(Unit)................................ (Accounting Period)..

Particulars.			Dripping, lbs.					Sales, lbs.							
Date.	Rations Drawn.	"B" "M" "S" "F" &c.	Saved.			Used for Cooking.		Issued in lieu of Margarine,	Dripping sold.			Butchers Fat.	Crack-lings, &c.	Bones.		Remarks.
			1st	2nd	Total.	1st	2nd	1st.	1st	2nd	Total.			Mar-row.	Others.	
																"B," "M," &c., is for beef, mutton, sausages, fish, &c. The column for dripping issues in lieu of margarine should be separated where messing is by companies. The form used should be the complete record of a full accounting period.

From 'Manual of Military Cooking and Dietary, 1918'.

To ensure that this process was well regulated, the 1910 Manual includes a form which is a 'Quartermaster's Daily Dripping Return'. This form breaks down the number of meals prepared for each unit on a daily basis for the month.[43] It has to be signed off every day and was clearly intended to prevent any 'skimming' to provide 'cook perks'.

NOTES ON SAVING WASTE FATS

If the ordinary waste water is thrown down the drain which in time become blocked owing to the fat cooling in the pipes, or it is passed through straw to prevent the fat from going into the drain or soak pit, in both cases a very valuable by product of the men's rations is wasted. In a certain unit in the command the following system for saving the fat has been adopted, with success and upwards of £40 has been realised by the sale of the same in 3 months.

A) 2 large second galvanised tanks were purchased and set up beside each other near a drain or soak pit and these are fitted at the bottom with a screw plug for drawing off the water in the drain or soak pit.

B) No washing up water is allowed to be put into the drain or soak pit direct, but is placed into the tanks to cool, and when cool the fat is taken off and the water which has been freed from fat is allowed to run into drain or soak pit.

C) This fat which of course will be found very dirty is clarified by boiling in a copper and is then ready for sale, it is then clean and white and paid for at the high rate of £44 per ton.

D) Before any table refuse is put into the swill tub it is carefully looked over by a man detailed for the purpose, whose duty it is to extract any bits of meat. This meat is melted down and put through a press, when all fat is extracted, leaving nothing but very dry scraps and crackling. This fat is also boiled and clarified, nothing in the way of grease is allowed to go down drains or into swill tubs, and it well repays the trouble taken in making the saving.

From Log Book of Cpl P.R. Froud, Feb. 1917

The level of supervision a cook received is made clear in 'Standing Orders of an Infantry Battalion, 1917'.[44] These standing orders were published as part of King's Regulations and were prepared in 1916 for the instruction of new or recently promoted officers and NCOs. The publication makes it clear that the NCO responsible for the cooks is the Sergeant Cook and that he is under the supervision of the Quartermaster. He is to supervise the work done in the battalion cookhouse and to ensure that it is both clean and secure. Great stress is placed on economical use of ingredients and fuel, combined with variety of diet. For this reason, an official form, R.F.10, was established, which details the diet to be provided for the three meals each day – breakfast, dinner and supper. This has to signed off by both the Sergeant Cook or Company Quartermaster Sergeant and the Second in Command of the Battalion or Company.[45] Corporal Froud trained as Master Cook in February 1917, and his Log Book provides additional detail about the responsibility of this post. He lists twenty-six 'Duties of the Master Cook'.[46]

DUTIES OF THE MASTER COOK

1) Care of and management of kitchens in camps, barracks, huts and billets. The cleanliness of himself and everybody in his charge.

2) Explanation of all apparatus and improvised appliance in general use.

3) Indenting for and drawing and issuing rations.

4) Jointing of meat and bacon, rest joints for baking purposes, frying, salting, etc. How to distinguish fresh and frozen. Good and bad. Old and young.

5) Telling off the messes and serving of food for some.

6) Cutting up and distribution of rations to the cooks in the cookhouse, joints and quantities necessary for the several diets.

7) A. Preparation of various dishes. Vegetables, Pastrys, Puddings etc.
B. Savories, Tomatoes, Ham, Anchovies, Eggs etc.
C. Entrees made up of 1) Cooked Meats 2) Fresh Meats.
D. Treatment of dried pulse that is Harricot beans, Peas, Butter Beans, etc. Dry fruit, prunes, apple rings, peaches, figs, fresh fruit for tarts, stewing etc. Tinned fish, various kinds of green vegetables.

E. Preparation and cooking of Beef Tea & Mutton Broth.

8) Treatment of bones, there [sic] uses and advantages in cooking.

9) Method of preparing stock, chief points of note.

10) Expressive fat from meat is used etc.

11) Stale Bread: A) How it can be used. B) How it can be used for bread crumbs.

12) Cold meat and how it can be made into hot dishes.

13) Pastry made with dripping, lard, suet etc.

14) Puddings suitable kinds for using of the stale bread, converting bread savings into flour.

15) How to make a brine tub and the particular joints to be pickled to advantage.

16) Preparation and cooking of preserved rations, preparation of food for invalids, making bread in the field.

17) Preparation of rissoles, brawn, potted meats.

18) Fish various kinds, reasons and methods of cooking. Quantities required etc.

19) Mess tin cooking, the erection of Aldershot Oven, improvised oven and kettle trenches, materials required for same how and where to erect them and how to work them.

20) Saving of dripping and clarifying use of stock pot.

21) Building trench ovens, improvised brazier and cooking in the same.

22) Thorough explanation of travelling kitchen. There use and advantages.

23) The use and methods of compiling AB48.A grocery slips and diet sheets.

24) Use and misuse of refuse tubs, sale of all by products to the best advantage.

25) Central messing and its advantages.

26) How to prevent waste of food and fuel at all times.

From Log Book of Cpl P.R. Froud, Feb. 1917

No. 6. **SPECIMEN DAY'S**

Meals.				Ingredients Required.	
				Free Issue.	Purchased.
BREAKFAST.	Tea.	Bread and Margarine.	Fried Bacon.	Tea, 1 lb. Sugar, 3¾ lbs. Bread as required Bacon, 25 lbs.	Milk, 5 pints Margarine, 3 lbs. 2 ozs. Pepper as required Mustard as required
DINNER.	Plain Stew.	Potatoes, Blue Peas.	Bread Pudding.	Meat, 62 lbs. Dripping, 3½ lbs. Bread as required Flour, 3 lbs. Sugar, 2 lbs. Sa.t as required	Potatoes, 50 lbs. Onions, 3 lbs. Mixed Root Vegs., 7 lbs. Currants or Prunes, 6 lbs. Mixed Peel, 1 lb. Spice, 2 ozs. Blue peas, 10 lbs. Pepper as required Mustard as required
TEA.	Tea,	Bread and	Margarine.	Mixed Salad.	Tea, 1 lb. Sugar, 3¾ lbs. Bread as required Salt as required	Milk, 5 pints Margarine, 3 lbs. 2 ozs. Beetroot, 15 lbs. Tomatoes, 4 lbs. Onions, 3 lbs. Vinegar, 2 pints Pepper as required
SUPPER.	*Vegetable Soup.	Bread.		Flour, 3 lbs. Bread as required Salt as required	Pearl Barley, 4 lbs. Mixed Root Vegs., 15 lbs. Onions, 3 lbs.

* Any spare cooked vegetables may be used in this preparation.

From 'Manual of Military Cooking and Dietary, 1918'.

DIET—100 Men.

Method of Preparation and Cooking.

As explained in Diet 2.

PLAIN STEW.—Wash, peel and cut up the vegetables into small cubes, clean and cut up the onions. Remove the meat from the bone and cut up into pieces of about 1 oz. Place 3 lbs. of flour, ½ oz. pepper, 3 ozs. salt, into a bowl and mix well, add the meat to this mixture. Place a little stock into a steaming dish or camp kettle, add the vegetables, onions and floured meat, barely cover with stock, stir well, replace the lid, and steam for 2½ to 3 hours. This should be occasionally stirred during process of cooking. If this stew is to be cooked in a camp kettle the meat should *not be floured* as above, but should be well whisked with stock and added as a thickening about 30 minutes before being required.

BLUE PEAS.—Soak 12 hours and cook until tender.

BREAD PUDDING.—Wash and pick over the currants, chop up the peel finely, and soak 25 lbs. bread in cold water for a few minutes ; then squeeze out all water, leaving the bread in a pulp. Place the currants, bread, peel, dripping, sugar and spice into a bowl and well mix. Well grease baking dishes, add the mixture, press into the dishes to a thickness of 2 ins., place in a moderately heated oven till cooked. Time, about 1 hour. This pudding can also be steamed. Prepare in same manner and place into a steaming dish, cover with the lid, and steam for 1½ hours.

MIXED SALAD.—Place the beetroot into boiling water without breaking the skins or removing any earth that may be adhering to them, and boil till tender. Time, old, 3 hours ; young, 1½ to 2 hours. When cooked remove from water and allow to cool. Remove the stalk and skin and cut up into thin slices. Remove the stalk from the tomatoes and wipe clean and cut in halves. Clean and ring the onions if large or remove the root and clean if spring onions. Lay the cut beetroot into plates or dishes, garnish with onions and tomatoes, and pour over the vinegar and serve.

VEGETABLE SOUP.—Scald the barley, prepare the vegetables and onions. Place barley into cold stock and simmer till cooked. Fry the vegetables and onions in a little dripping, add to the stock. Make a thickening as explained in Diet 1, bring stock to the boil, add the thickening, and stir till cooked. Time for soup, about 3 hours.

The Army Book (A.B.) 48 A he refers to is the daily messing account, which showed what food was received and purchased. One surprising feature of the management of the mess is that the Messing Officer, who is neither a cook nor with the Quartermaster's Department, is assisted by a Messing Committee who are selected from the ranks every month. This committee are formally paraded to be given the opportunity to express grievances and to offer any suggestions relating to the diet sheet. It is worthy of note that Corporal Froud includes the observation: 'The diet must be good and varied, no fish to be served twice during one week'.[47]

ARMY BOOK FORM 48A

Army Book Form 48 A is the daily messing account, it shows what food is drawn and used and how it is used, it also shows what rations are on hand, one side of the sheet is used for the issue and the other for the purchased goods, there is another white slip called the field statement which as a rule the Sergt Cook indents on for the purchase goods. The following days groceries have been indented for the slip is handed to the grocery bar manager. The mess book is generally kept by one man in each unit unless company messing. The general control is effected by a messing officer who is not in any way connected with the Quartermasters Dept. This officer is assisted by a messing committee who are selected from the ranks every month and are paraded in front of the messing officer to ventilate any grievance and to offer any suggestions. The Sergt Cook usually compiles the Diet Sheet for the week and should be present at the monthly mess meeting. The Quartermaster generally indents for the free issue 3 days in advance. The 48 A gives the required amount to spend so the company or battalion does not get into debt.

Things to note when compiling a diet sheet:

1) The diet must be good and varied, no fish to be served twice during one week.
2) No two dishes containing the same ingredients should be served at one meal.
3) The value of various foods should be studied.
4) Greens and vegetables should be given in fair proportions, also salads when in season.

5) The diet should be arranged so that the men have a roast one day and a stew the next.

6) The following must be considered, price of material, the money to be expended, the taste of the men and the times when different articles are in season. Watch for a glut of any article on the market in order to buy them cheaply.

7) It should also be taken into consideration that any surplus meat, bread etc is available from the previous day for inclusion on the diet.

From Log Book of Cpl P.R. Froud, Feb. 1917

Concerning his experience of rations whilst in training at Aldershot, Private William St Clair wrote home in 1916:

We are being fed fairly decent but are hard up for knives and forks. My pocket knife has had to do everything. We drink the stew out of our cups up to now, plates being at a premium. The food is well cooked. So we get outside of it as best as we can.[48]

Private Leveratt would have been familiar with the regulations as they are laid out in the book and he would have had chance to put some of these into action between the end of his training and embarkation for the front. His Pension Record reveals that Private Leveratt was sent to France on 16 April 1917, but that his service career was brief. He was appointed a lance corporal on 13 May, but was then wounded on or about 31 May. At the time, the various battalions of the Worcester Regiment were not involved in battle, but some were in the line. We can therefore presume that he was wounded by shellfire, possibly even when working as a cook. He was returned to Britain for treatment on 22 June. He was later medically downgraded and transferred to the Royal Defence Force, the Great War version of the Home Guard. Sadly his wounds meant that he had to be discharged from the forces in late November 1917. In return for his services, he received a Silver War Badge that was to be worn with civilian clothes to indicate that despite no visible wounds he was a disabled serviceman.[49] At the end of the war, he was in receipt of a pension, although the records do not indicate the nature of his disability. If Corporal Leveratt's record is typical, it indicates that being an army cook was not a safe option, however brief your service life.

ARMY COOK'S TIP NO.3

Rub the hands on a stick of celery after peeling onions, and the smell will be entirely removed.

From Log Book of G.N.R. Smith, 368 Siege Battery, RGA

To get a better indication of life at the front for a cook, Private Dolden's memoir is a rare and detailed account. He reports that, whilst at Laventie, while one cook remained with the company cooker:

> The other cooks separated and each went with a platoon into line. Our dixies etc., were carried by carried by the platoon ... the platoon was put into two wooden huts, and two wooden huts, and close by there was a little wooden cookhouse, over which I reigned supreme ...

Although able to sleep in the cookhouse he clearly had a late evening and, presumably, an early start.

> After having lit a fire, I went round to the other posts to see how the cooks were getting on. When I returned I made tea for the boys, and then retired to my billet for the night.

If he had the advantage of a cosy billet for the night, he would also be up well before dawn to light the fires for tea and to prepare breakfast for the less fortunate members of the company, who would have worked or been on guard duty all night. In the day that followed, the routine for the cooks would have been as demanding in the field as in camp, and short-ages of fuel and rations, combined with enemy action and the weather, would make the task even more difficult. Despite these circumstances, even under field conditions, Private Dolden and fellow cooks were able to improvise a 'Burns Night' supper for his unit, the London Scottish, when they came out of the line:

> We cooked the haggis in a large bath tub. The dinner took place at 3.20pm and the menu was: Soup, Roast Beef and Onions, Haggis, Plum Duff, Desert ... and Rum Punch.[50]

Food was not always of this quality, however, and the cooks were not always at fault:

> When the meat arrived next day its presence was so obvious that we had suspicions as to its goodness. We accordingly got the MO to have a look at it. He condemned part of it, and the rest we had to wash in permanganate of potash. [51]

Quite what even the best cook could do to make stinking meat, which had been washed in chemicals, taste palatable is open to debate. What is certain, however, is that it would be the cooks that would get the blame. Even when they prepared food, the cooks could get into trouble with the men they were feeding, because of problems getting the meal down the line:

> [On 2 September 1916] the battalion moved off. The dixies filled with meat and vegetables were handed to the Platoon to carry, and they were far from keen on the job, and at 3.45 we left Drucat. In the darkness the sound of Dixie lids falling off could be heard, accompanied by a good deal of cursing from those carrying them.[52]

What condition the rations were in when they arrived in the frontline can only be a matter of speculation. The dixie lids would have fallen in the mud and been replaced at various times during the journey up the trenches. The various attempts to replace them in the dark would have introduced a large amount of non-ration material to the mix. For the men serving and eating in the dark, the result of discovering that what was being eaten was at best mud can be well imagined. They would, of course, blame the cooks, not the men of the clumsy carrying party! The importance of food to men who had been in action is illustrated by the experience of a soldier in the London Rifle Brigade in 1915.

After nine days in the frontline, the unit was relieved and made its way to the rear:

At last we entered a field where our cookers were drawn up, and a very sympathetic party of cooks, transport-drivers and QMSs stood there ready to wait on us 'hand and foot'.[53]

ARMY COOK'S TIP NO.4

When beating eggs be careful to see that there is no grease of any kind on the whisk, or it will prevent the eggs from frothing.

From Log Book of G.N.R. Smith, 368 Siege Battery, RGA, May 1917

As we have learnt from Private Leveratt's experience, being an army cook was never a guarantee of an easy life or indeed safety. Private Dolden describes a situation when he was behind the lines, but where conditions were far from ideal:

Profiting by previous experience, we placed the cooker behind a brick wall to avoid being hit by machine gun bullets which had a habit of whistling past us as we were working ... One night Macpherson, a fellow cook, was standing on the cooker attending to the dixies when a machine gun bullet ricocheted off the cooker chimney. Much too close for his liking ... The mud was so thick that we obtained three trench boards from the Royal engineer's dump to place round the cooker. Trench boards were similar to a wooden ladder with slats to allow the water to drain off and so did not get buried in the mud.[54]

By 1918, aerial bombing was a threat to men, even well behind the lines, and an attack by a German raider ruined breakfast for a full company when the battalion was housed in a hutted camp:

The cookers were standing about seventeen feet away from the shed, but pieces of bomb had hit ours in several places. One of the wheels, and also the supporting pole, was cut in two. Dixies were punctured, and metal bowls and knives twisted up like paper. The whole Battalion rations were destroyed, and the Quartermaster had to telephone the ASC dump for more. We had cut up about one hundred and fifty rashers of bacon for the Company's breakfast, but these were nowhere to be seen.[55]

Another company cook was not so fortunate and in early 1918 he records that: 'The next day was Good Friday. The first news I heard was that poor "Tich" Davidson, a D Company cook, had been blown to pieces by a shell ...'.[56]

It was not just enemy action that made a cook's life difficult and dangerous. During the harsh winter of 1916–17, Private Dolden's unit was out of the line:

We spent five days in that position, during which the cold grew gradually more intense. One morning when Davidson and I got up to make breakfast, we found everything frozen. The lids were tight on the dixies, and our bread as hard as a rock. A pot of syrup was as solid as toffee, and we had to break the ice on the neighbouring stream to obtain water ... On one occasion I took a dixie of boiling water off the fire and stood it six feet away from the blaze, and with half an hour it was frozen hard. The tea in our mugs became a solid mass; and we began to realise the hardships of a winter campaign.[57]

On another occasion, an attempt to provide a hot drink for men in the line had tragic consequences:

One evening 'Digger' and I had just made tea for the boys; to make carrying easier, this had as usual been poured into petrol tins. These were left in the cookhouse till the carrying party came for them. Unfortunately they were placed too near the fire, and one of them began to boil. To prevent it from bursting, and so probably wreck the cookhouse, I went to unscrew the metal stopper. There was a tremendous rush of scalding tea, which caught me on the right side of the face. I ducked, and the boiling steam rushed down my back and right shoulder. I then dropped to the floor; by this time the boiling tea was hitting the roof of the cookhouse, so that by dropping I got out of range. The pain was awful so I ripped off my shirt and immediately rushed outside in the cool, as the heat from the fire made the pain unbearable. 'Digger', with great presence of mind, rubbed the whole of the twenty-four hour butter ration over my burns. It happened to be salted butter and I gave a frantic leap ... The next day may face was swollen and my back was raw, and it was only by a fraction of an inch that my right eye was missed ... [58]

ARMY COOK'S TIP NO.5

To render pork sausages more digestible, thoroughly prick the sausages and plunge into boiling water for 5 minutes. Then fry the usual way. This is the proper way to cook sausages.

From the Log Book of G.N.R. Smith, 368 Siege Battery, RGA

We cannot be certain that Private Dolden's trials and adventures were typical for an army cook in the Great War, but they do stand to indicate the problems and dangers that they faced. They also illustrate that being a cook, at least for a frontline unit, was not necessarily a 'cushy billet' in time of war. As the war progressed, male cooks were joined by women volunteers who worked as VADs in a variety of hospitals and camps, and later by the members of the Women's Army Auxiliary Corps (WAACs). Although officially classified as 'camp followers', members of the corps took on a range of domestic and clerical duties, and this included cooking. One feature of this transition was that the jobs previously undertaken by men were taken over by women, releasing them for more active duties. It is perhaps not surprising that some men resented the arrival of women, not because they wanted to keep women out of the war, but because the wanted to keep 'their' jobs. One interesting feature of male cooks, however, is the question of whether they told their families how they had spent the war. One can imagine that a combination of the fear of being judged to have avoided frontline duty, together with that of avoiding future culinary activities in the domestic kitchen, would produce a certain reluctance to discuss the nature of 'their' war. Perhaps the answer to the question 'Daddy, what did you do in the war?' being 'I don't want to talk about it' had more to do with avoiding kitchen duties rather than protecting the family from the horrors of war?

A Typical Army Cook: Private Abel Flitney

WE ARE FORTUNATE that Private Dolden included his job as a cook in his memoirs. The vast majority of men similarly employed left no such record and we can only reconstruct their culinary career from the scant evidence they left behind.

A typical example is Abel Flitney, a wartime volunteer who must have read about stirring bayonet charges in the newspapers before he found himself actually stirring stew. When the Great War broke out Abel Flitney was 38 years old and a gardener living near Sevenoaks in Kent. He was married to Matilda and had two daughters. The eldest, aged 10, was Rhoda and the other, Margaret, was just 6.[59] By 1915, he was in uniform as Private G/12022 Flitney, A., and in the ranks of the 13th Battalion, The Royal Sussex Regiment.[60]

At some stage between joining up and 1916, Abel was sent to the school of cookery at Portslade near Brighton in Sussex. By pure good fortune, the illustrated cookery Log Book that he compiled in the camp has survived and is now in the collection of The Royal Logistic Corps Museum.[61] The Log Book gives a great deal of detail about the nature of his training and the attention to detail makes interesting reading. On page one of the log, a simple exercise book, he wrote out notes from a lecture or possibly those on a black board. His first entry is 'Method of Preparation and Cooking' and this continues with the information that 'Dripping, Bones, Crackling, etc … these things are all used for making high explosive or soap or many other things useful for the progress of war'.

At the conclusion of his course, which was usually around six weeks, Private Flitney would have been posted back to his unit. At that time, the battalion was in Britain, so the budding cook would have had a gentle introduction to his new trade. Permanent camp cookhouses in a hutted camp would have given him time to put into practice all the lessons learned at Portslade. We cannot be certain what the men of the Royal Sussex Regiment made of Abel's cookery, however it is clear that even the worst cooks could turn out popular meals, especially with younger recruits. George Coppard reports:

> The battalion cooks got busy with the field-kitchens, and life began to glow in us with the sweet smell of bacon frying. A familiar cry I loved to

A Good Book & a good man would make a good cook Signed by Instructor Jermy. S of C Portslade

no 12022

Pte A Flitney
3rd Royal Sussex Regt
School of Cookery
Portslade

Method of Preparation and Cooking

Cleanliness with all Utensils
By Products

Dripping Bones Cracklings Ete these things are used for makeing high explosive or soap or many other things useful for the progress of War,

Dripping Bones are worth £ £8 per ton
Bones   "   "   "   £6n" — —
Dry Bones and marrow   £7 " — —
cracklings If pressed   £3 " 10 — —
If not Pressed   £9 " 10 — —

One mans rashon of meat, cook should save 1 oz of dripping per day & not less than ½ oz a cook

From Log Book of Pte A. Flitney.

The gravestone of military cook, Pte A. Flitney, 3rd Royal Sussex Regiment, School of Cookery, Portslade.

G/12022 PRIVATE
A. FLITNEY
ROYAL SUSSEX REGIMENT
2ND AUGUST 1917 AGE 39

FLING OPEN WIDE
THE GOLDEN GATES
AND LET THE VICTOR IN

hear was 'Roll up for your dip!' This was the hot swimming bacon fat in which one could dip a slice of bread. Experience told me to drop everything and run like hell to get in quick. Sometimes the cooks poured an extra tin of condensed milk into the big dixies of tea. The toffee-like brew seemed delicious to my young palate.[62]

Abel's battalion was part of 116th Brigade in 39th Division and went to France, via Le Havre, in March 1916. It is very likely that he was with them when they arrived on the continent and during the heavy fighting on the Somme from September to November of that year. Casualties were heavy and by 10 November, 50 per cent of the officers and 66 per cent of the Other Ranks were reinforcements replacing the dead and wounded of the preceding few months of bitter fighting. The casualties were so heavy that the division was withdrawn to refit and train the reinforcements that had arrived to replace those lost in action.[63] The battalion did not go into battle again until 31 July 1917 at Ypres, at the beginning of the battle which would become known as Passchendaele. The sector allocated to the 116th Brigade for the attack was east of the city of Ypres in the area of Forward Cottage. By the end of the day, the 13th Battalion had captured the village of St Julien and taken seventeen German officers and 205 Other Ranks prisoner.[64] It is not clear what role Private Flitney played in this success. Whether as a cook waiting to move forward with the cookers to the captured objective to serve hot meals or, as is very possible, as an infantryman to bolster the number of experienced men in the line. It is clear that he was wounded and evacuated to one of the dressing stations on the edge of Ypres. His death is recorded on 2 August and he is buried in La Brique Military Cemetery No. 2.[65] A poignant reminder of the life and death of this army cook is a photograph of his headstone in the cemetery that was pasted into the front cover of his cookery Log Book by one of his family. The family had paid 3½ old pence per letter for the private inscription 'Fling Open Wide The Golden Gates And Let The Victors In'.[66] The total cost of this final gesture for a husband and father would have been over 14s, two weeks' wages for a private soldier.

THE ARMY RATION

IF ONE USES the standard sources of information about the nature of rations issued to British troops on the Western Front, it is very easy to produce examples of bad rations that were poorly cooked, missing meals and endless accounts of 'bully beef and biscuit' in the frontline. The fact that at least half the army was not infantry, and therefore never went into the trenches, is ignored, as is the fact that even infantrymen were not permanently in the trenches. The universal experience for soldiers from their first day in recruit training to their worst day in action was eating meals which consisted of the issue rations supplemented by food they purchased with their own money. Clearly not all of these meals would be well cooked and the soldier's reaction to them would depend upon their diet at home and personal taste. It is therefore very instructive to contrast military rations with standard meals in Britain for the labouring men, who would form the bulk of the manpower of the British forces during the war. A book published in 1911, *British Rural Life and Labour*, provides excellent comparative figures. The average amount of beef or mutton consumed per week by each family was 3lb 6oz and bacon 2lb 11½oz. The average amount of bread eaten by a family was 19½lb, and potatoes just over 25lb. This was meant to feed a family of two adults and one or more children.

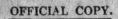

ARMY RATIONS: THEIR BEARING ON THE EFFICIENCY OF THE SOLDIER.

D. NOËL PATON, M.D., F.R.S.,

PROFESSOR OF PHYSIOLOGY, UNIVERSITY OF GLASGOW.

LONDON:
PUBLISHED BY HIS MAJESTY'S STATIONERY OFFICE.

To be purchased through any Bookseller or directly from
H.M. STATIONERY OFFICE at the following addresses:
IMPERIAL HOUSE, KINGSWAY, LONDON, W.C. 2, and 28, ABINGDON STREET, LONDON, S.W. 1;
37, PETER STREET, MANCHESTER; 1, ST. ANDREW'S CRESCENT, CARDIFF;
23, FORTH STREET, EDINBURGH;
or from E. PONSONBY, LTD,, 116, GRAFTON STREET, DUBLIN.

Price 3d. Net.

ARMY RATIONS: THEIR BEARING ON THE EFFICIENCY OF THE SOLDIER.

D. NOËL PATON, M.D., F.R.S.,
Professor of Physiology, University of Glasgow.

Napoleon is credited with the saying that an Army marches on its stomach. It is a picturesque way of expressing that the work which the soldier can do depends upon the food which he eats, and that all his energy comes from his food, and that if he is to fight well he must be well fed.

It is the duty of every officer to know this and to bear it constantly in mind. He should also recognise that not only must energy-yielding food be provided, but that before the energy can be used the food must be digested and absorbed. Hence he must know something of the processes of digestion, under what conditions they proceed normally and how they are apt to be disturbed.

In considering the feeding of the soldier, two distinct questions have thus to be dealt with.

1. The uses and values of food.

2. The digestion and mode of utilisation of food in the body.

I.—THE USES AND VALUE OF FOOD.

It must be constantly kept in mind that the great purpose of food is to supply energy—the power of doing work. Just as the work-doing power of an engine comes from the combustion of the coals in the furnace or of petrol in the cylinder, so the work-doing power of a man comes from the combustion of his food in his body. The energy for the engine is stored in the coal or petrol—the energy for the man is stored in his food.

As every one knows, all the energy in the world comes from the sun. Green plants are the instruments for the storage of that energy. Those of past æons stored it and gradually became converted into coal, from which the energy is liberated in the process of burning. A field of wheat is simply an apparatus for storing solar energy. After the wheat has been made into bread and eaten, the energy is set free in the body; or it may be first consumed by cattle or pigs, in which case only a small part of the energy of the grain is stored in the flesh and made available for man when the flesh is eaten.

(B 14459) A 2

From 'Army Rations: Their Bearing on the Efficiency of the Soldier'.

'The British Army Service Corps at Work'. Fearless of danger, the Army Service Corps regularly carried out their work of feeding men in the firing line, often themselves going up to the men and giving them rations. From a picture by A.C. Michael. (Author's collection)

Pre-war army manoeuvres: the logistics of feeding the First World War army was borne out of practice and preparation. Here we see a field bakery being created to make sure the men were honed in the skills that they would have to put to use in the front. (RLC Museum)

This jolly postcard gives a rather more cheerful view of what it was like to run a field bakery than would have been the case on the Western Front. (RLC Museum)

Getting supplies to the Front was a huge challenge in man and motor power. Here we see supplies being unloaded at a dock side. (RLC Museum)

The next step on their journey: a huge park of motor lorries waiting at a railhead to load up supplies. (RLC Museum)

Interior of the Expeditionary Force Canteen Store, Cologne. (RLC Museum)

At the British ration dump, Cologne, 14 February 1919. (RLC Museum)

A top view of a travelling kitchen; note the various cooking compartments and water supply tap. (RLC Museum)

Spanish generals visit the Western Front, inspecting bread at a bakery in Rouen, March 1917. (RLC Museum)

Lunch at the Front. This gives a good indication of how field kitchens in practice look.

Lunch on the move. This type of improvised cooking would be a part of life when moving to and from the Front.

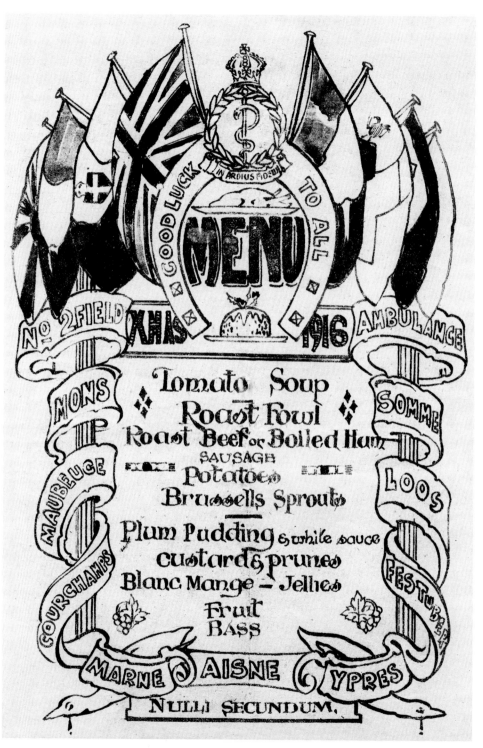

This extremely rare menu shows how No.2 Field Ambulance celebrated Christmas 1916 – not a bad meal! (Author's collection)

ARMY COOK'S TIP NO.6

To Clean a Water Bottle

Place into the water bottle a small quantity of tea leaves, and a small lump salt. Pour in about one third of a teacupful of vinegar, shake well, empty and rinse with cold water.
If glass a perfectly clear glass will result.

From Log Book of G.N.R. Smith, 368 Siege Battery, RGA

The book also contained typical daily menus for labouring families from various British counties. The menu for the area around Ely in Cambridgeshire provides an interesting contrast to army rations, and is not the worst menu described:

Breakfast. – Tea with sugar, no milk: bread, butter, or lard. The man probably has a herring or a small piece of pork.
Dinner. – Potatoes fried in lard, or pudding with pork and onions on it, potatoes (Sunday, fresh beef or pork).
Tea. – Tea with sugar, no milk: bread and butter or lard.
Supper. – Bread and scraps left over from dinner.[67]

By comparison, a soldier's ration of meat for a week can be calculated as 8¾lb per man and the same weight in bread. He also received 1lb 5oz of bacon and 3½lb of vegetables.[68] In other words, he was personally issued with more than twice the meat, half the bacon and bread, and roughly a third of the vegetables a family would consume in a week. This means that a soldier received at least as much, and probably more, protein in the army than he did at home and his only reduction was vegetables that had previously provided a large bulk of his diet. Although it is arguable that some men in more well-paid trades did a great deal better, it must also be recalled that many men were under or unemployed in 1914. With no Welfare State system this meant 'the bread line' and semi-starvation for many families. By contrast, a soldier who was not satisfied with his regular, if uninspiring rations, could supplement his food with his wage. It must also be recalled that these calculations are based on the rations issued in Britain for soldiers in training and there were circumstances in which, closer to the front or in the trenches, not all the stipulated rations were issued. However, taking these figures as a base line and working from what was meant to be issued we can calculate, rather more accurately than many memoirs, what was actually issued, if not eaten. Critically, soldiers were all paid in local currency and in a position to purchase additional food when they were not in action. Men at home with no regular income simply went hungry, as did their families.

At the outbreak of war the scale of rations issued to troops at home was:

Bread	1¼lb
Meat	1¼lb
Tea	5/8oz
Sugar	3oz
Salt	½oz
Pepper	1/36oz
Mustard	1/20oz
Jam	4oz
Bacon	4oz
Cheese	3oz
Fresh Vegetables	8oz[69]

This was calculated to produce a total of 4,607 calories per day. This can be compared to an average working man's 3,400 per day at home. The scale of rations was reduced at various points in the war, initially in August and September 1914, and then in each successive year of the war. However, as the issued food was reduced, a daily cash allowance was introduced and gradually increased so that the soldier could purchase his own 'extras'. One complaint that was made throughout the war and by soldiers in later conflicts was the lack of choice provided by a fix scale of rations. Offering cash provided an element of choice that would not have been otherwise possible. The cash allowance eventually increased to 6½d specifically for young, and growing, soldiers and those involved in demanding work or training. As the pay at this period for a private soldier was 1s (12d) per day this sum of money had considerable purchasing power. That said, the War Office and the Royal Army Medical Corps appear to have been involved in a balancing act when it came to an adequate diet, as food shortages caused problems on the home front. Soldiers rarely went short, but distinctions between the requirements of growing boys and those involved in sedentary activities continued to be made. One shortage that did lead to complaint was a shortage of meat. The 8oz of meat provided daily in 1918 was considered insufficient, as was the provision of bacon for breakfast – only four times a week.[70] To put this in perspective it is instructive to look at Army Book 14. 'Ready Reckoned for Field Rations'.[71] This indicates that a 2oz breakfast of bacon would amount to a total of 125lb for 1,000 men per day. A ration of 8oz of meat daily would constitute 500lb for the same number of men every day.

On the outbreak of war, the scale of Field Rations was divided into bread, meat, and a grocery ration:

Bread	1¼lb
or	
Biscuit	¾lb
Fresh or frozen meat	1¼lb
or	
Preserved meat	1lb
Tea	⅝oz
Sugar	3oz
Salt	½oz
Pepper	¹⁄₃₆oz
Mustard	¹⁄₂₀oz
Jam	4oz
Bacon	4oz
Cheese	3oz
Fresh Vegetables	8oz
or	
Dried Vegetables	2oz[72]

In addition, there were allowances of butter or margarine, oatmeal, rice, milk and pickles. This provides 4,495 calories: a figure that would reduce throughout the war, although the low point was the early part of 1917 when submarine warfare greatly reduced the quantity of food that could be shipped to the Continent from the Empire and other sources of supply.

Field Rations
Daily ration for a British Soldier in summer 1917

Meat (fresh or frozen)	1lb
or	
Meat (preserved) Bully Beef	9oz
Bread	1lb
or	
Biscuit	10oz
Bacon	4oz
Cheese	2oz
Fresh Vegetables	8oz
or	
Dried Vegetables	2oz
Tea	5/8oz
Jam (plum and apple)	3oz
Butter	2oz
Sugar	3oz
Oatmeal (three times a week)	2oz
Rice	1oz
Salt	¼oz
Mustard	1/100oz
Pepper	1/100oz
Milk (condensed)	1oz
Pickles (weekly)	1oz[73]

From April 1917, a ration for Line of Communication (LoC) Troops, who were not expected to engage in combat, was introduced. This reduced the quantity of rations provided for these troops and provided them with roughly 3,500 calories compared to the 4,500 of the rest of the army.[74] It must, however, be recalled that any troops behind the lines, whether in a training camp, hospital or on the Lines of Communication, were able to supplement their rations with purchases from the Expeditionary Force Canteens, the forerunner of NAAFI, and organisations such as the

Red Cross, YMCA, etc. These soldiers would also be able to pay for food and drink from the local population. This opportunity was, of course, also available to frontline troops as they rotated through 'resting', training, or being held in reserve before returning for a spell in the line.

In case of emergency the soldier also carried on him his 'Iron Ration' which comprised '1lb of preserved meat; 12oz of biscuit, 5/8oz of tea; 2oz of sugar; ½oz of salt; 3oz of cheese and two cubes of meat extract'.[75] To ensure that even if the normal supply system was interrupted, the British Army had a system of Reserve Park made up of units of the Army Service Corps, which carried two days' reserve of Iron Rations, along with groceries for the men and two days' oats for the horses in a division. Groceries included tea, sugar, tinned milk, bacon, jam and cheese.[76] As the official history of The Royal Army Service Corps makes clear:

> It could not be calculated that for a European War the Army could subsist on preserved rations and, as local supplies would be obviously inadequate for any large force over any long period, the transport formations would need to be organised for maintenance wholly from the rear.[77]

Rations were, therefore, intended to be issued on a daily basis to men via the General Scheme of Supply. In this system, rations and other items were sent from bases established in major ports such as Calais, Boulogne and Rouen where shipping could unload and stocks could be kept. The combination of different supplies were sent by rail to a Regulating Station on what was known, at the time, as the Lines of Communication (LoC). Here the various amount of commodities for the variety of units and their different strengths was calculated, so that the 'Divisional Pack Trains' that were sent forward to the railhead were appropriately loaded with a combination of rations, fodder for animals, fuel and ammunition.[78]

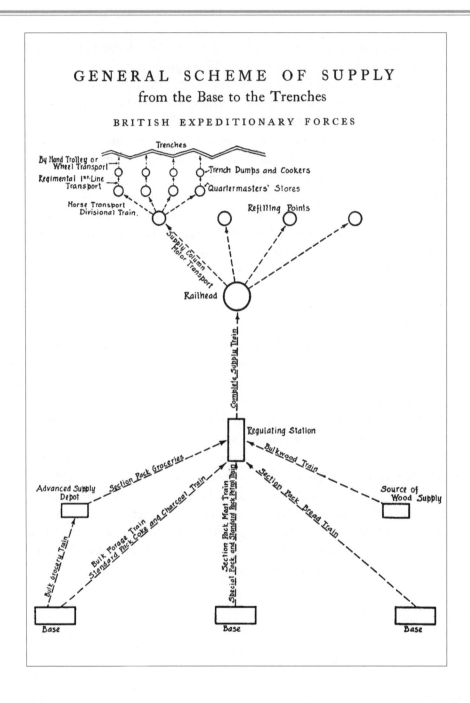

GENERAL SCHEME OF SUPPLY
from the Base to the Trenches

BRITISH EXPEDITIONARY FORCES

Trenches

By Hand Trolley or Wheel Transport — Trench Dumps and Cookers

Regimental 1st-Line Transport — Quartermasters' Stores

Horse Transport Divisional Train.

Refilling Points

Supply Column Motor Transport

Railhead

Complete Supply Train

Regulating Station

Bulkwood Train

Section Pack Groceries

Advanced Supply Depot

Bulk Forage Train
Standard Pack Coke and Charcoal Train

Special Section Pack Meat Train and Standard Pack Petrol Train

Section Pack Bread Train

Source of Wood Supply

Bulk Grocery Train

Base

Base

Base

FUEL

It will be obvious that a careful and economical use of fuel will be necessary, in order to carry out the system of messing as now approved. It has been practically demonstrated that with careful supervision, the regulation allowance is barely sufficient to meet all requirements, the following remarks are issued for information on this subject:

1) The allowance of coal for the cookhouse should be issued daily to the Sergeant Cook & care should be taken that an undue amount of slack is not included.

2) The Sergeant Cook will be held responsible for the economical consumption of coal, and it will be his duty to regulate the fires using no more than are necessary for the cooking required, by consulting the Regimental Diet return, the Sergeant Cook will be able to arrange beforehand how his cooking apparatus can be used to the best advantage.

3) Cinders should be carefully preserved as in some cases they are as valuable for fuel as coal.

4) The following rules should be observed:

a. Fires should not be kept burning longer than necessary, for instance, when soup has reached its boiling point a portion of the fire should be withdrawn, also when the brick ovens are heated to the required heat, the fire should be at once removed & the food cooked by the stored heat.

b. After fires have been used, but are required subsequently, they should be banked up by placing damp cinders on them, & the ashpit door & damper closed, leaving only sufficient draught to carry away the smoke, the furnace door being kept open.

c. In replenishing a fire, the live coal should be pushed to the back of the furnace, the fresh coal being added in front by so doing the fresh coal becomes gradually consumed & the heat of the fire is not reduced.

From Log Book of Pte A. Flitney, No. 1 2022, 3rd Royal Sussex Regt, School of Cookery, Portslade

At the railhead, which was as close to the frontline as possible, the train's contents were loaded onto lorries or, during the earlier part of the war, on horse transport. Based on the actual experience of trench warfare, the history of the RASC described how this was achieved on a daily basis for the entire duration of the war:

> Horsed supply wagons filled daily with fresh provisions at a distance of some forty miles from the railhead, thus making a 'turn-round' of eighty miles which could be taken as the maximum.[79]

If this sounds daunting, the history describes the situation should a corps of three divisions be advancing on a single route:

> There might well be some three divisions or some sixty thousand men and eighteen thousand animals on one road which would involve a distance of forty-five miles from front to rear. [80]

In static warfare, which was common for the majority of the Great War, rations and supplies were taken forward from the railhead at 'Refilling Points', first to divisional level on what was termed the 'Second-Line, Divisional, Transport' and then on to the regiment on the 'First Line Transport'. The rations would be regulated by the unit Quartermaster, who organized the last stage in this relay. The final step for rations was up to the cooks and cookers and then by manpower, or even light railway, up to the frontline for consumption. It must be noted that as only a fraction of the manpower of the BEF was actually in the frontline at any one time, the vast majority of the rations and other stores were consumed behind the lines.[81]

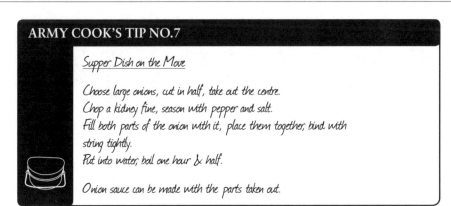

ARMY COOK'S TIP NO.7

Supper Dish on the Move

Choose large onions, cut in half, take out the centre.
Chop a kidney fine, season with pepper and salt.
Fill both parts of the onion with it, place them together, bind with
string tightly.
Put into water, boil one hour & half.

Onion sauce can be made with the parts taken out.

From Log Book of G.N.R. Smith, 368 Siege Battery, RGA

In terms of the pure bulk of food required each day, the 1914 Field Service Manual calculates that a battalion of 1,000 men would require:

> 1,007lb of biscuits and the same of preserved meat, 251lb of bacon, 188lb of cheese, 672lb of oats,
> 125lb of dried vegetables, 252lb of Jam and a total of 71lb of Tea, Sugar, Salt and Pepper plus 25 pints of Lime Juice, 126 pints of Rum and 18lb of tobacco per day in addition to other rations. [82]

The total weight, even if the calculation is based on a reduced scale of biscuit, rather than bread, preserved rather than fresh meat and dried vegetables, is 3,537lb – over 1½ Imperial tons (2½ metric tons) per 1,000 men. Based on a BEF in 1918 of 2⅓ million men this becomes a minimum of 563,7000 metric tons every day. As the load capacity of the standard General Service (GS) Wagon was around 2,700lb it is easy to calculate that a single battalion on bread, fresh meat and vegetables requires two GS wagons for rations alone, without drinking water, forage for horses and ammunition. As a calculation for the entire BEF, this becomes an overwhelming figure, which stretched the organisational capacity of the British Army throughout the war. The fact that rations did not always arrive or that some men went short should not surprise us.

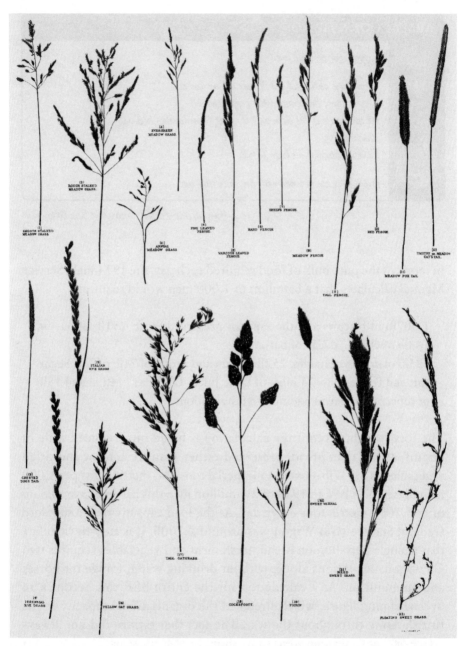

Taken from the 'Army Service Corps Training Manual Part II' (1914). All military cooks were trained in the art of foraging in order to ensure that their horses were kept well-fed. The manual includes a number of pull-outs like this that illustrate edible and inedible grasses.

FORAGING

Foraging was vital for keeping horses fed at the Front and the 'Army Service Corps Training Manual, Part III, 1909' contains an extensive section on foraging illustrated by detailed pull-outs identifying various types of grains and grasses:

'"Forage" includes all articles consumed as food by horses, mules, ponies &c. Certain substances used for bedding must also be considered, and are usually included in the term.

To be a good judge of forage is one of the most important duties of every officer belonging to a mounted corps, as its quality governs to a great extent the condition of the horses, and on this largely depends the amount of work which may be got out of them.

An officer's training requires him to approach the study of forage in a somewhat artificial manner; as practical experience of the subject will probably have been small, this must be compensated for by theoretical study.'

The section goes on to detail how an officer may ascertain which grains and grasses are appropriate and how these can be best used.

What is surprising, however, is the range of food provided, at least in theory, and the amount of protein represented by the meat ration, whether fresh or preserved. There was, on paper, no vegetarian option. However, the British Army had to cater for a wide range of nationalities and diets, and provision was made for a ration scale suitable for Indian personnel, which included mixed spices of ginger, turmeric, chillies and garlic, Dhal (lentils) and Attar (Wheat flour). Vegetarians received additional Gur (cane sugar) or milk instead of meat. Other variations were produced for the Chinese Labour Corps and Egyptian Labour Corps, Fijian Labourers, prisoners of war and, of course, those in hospitals. Specialist rations also had to be produced for Egypt, Macedonia, East Africa, Mesopotamia and, ultimately, North Russia.

The chapter on 'Supply of Food in the Trenches' in the *Official History of the Great War, Medical Services, Hygiene of the War* provides an illuminating account of the importance of hot rations to men in the trenches:

> The harmful effects of exposure and the resulting occurrence of trench foot were to some extent counteracted by the liberal ration and the means adopted for ensuring a daily supply of hot food. [83]

If this did not always occur, it was clearly not on the best advice of the officers in the Royal Army Medical Corps who were responsible for the health and wellbeing of the troops. One interesting fact the *Official History* reveals that men in the trenches received an additional ½oz of tea and ¾oz of sugar per day in addition to the normal ration scale. This, apparently, 'served a double purpose, in that not only was extra stimulant available, but it necessitated the water used being boiled when made into tea'.

As has already been seen, the 1914 ration scale included 1½lb of fresh meat or 1lb of preserved meat per day. The most popular meat, and the most economical to transport, was beef, but mutton provided a welcome alternative. Once the conflict had resolved itself into trench warfare it was apparent that fresh meat could not be prepared in frontline positions and therefore the men would have to eat preserved meat, which was largely corned beef or 'bully'. The Handbook of Specifications for Supplies, 1915 makes interesting reading when it comes to 'preserved meat'. The contract states that bully beef should be made from:

> ... the carcasses of cattle in prime condition not under two or over four years of age ... Each 12 oz. tin to contain not more than 1/2 oz., and each 24 oz. tin not more than 1 oz., of clear jelly made from soup stock and soup bones.[84]

The problem was that this ration rapidly became boring when issued for a prolonged period. The consequence of this was waste and the result was the decision to reduce the amount of meat issued per day and to some extent replace it by an issue of condensed milk. When British solders traded bully beef with the French their reaction to the contents of the tins was that it was '*singe*', or monkey.

Gen. No.

HANDBOOK

OF

SPECIFICATIONS FOR SUPPLIES.

GOVERNMENT LABORATORY
14 FEB. 1916
CLEMENT'S INN PASSAGE, STRAND, W.C.

WAR OFFICE.

1915.

LONDON:
PRINTED FOR HIS MAJESTY'S STATIONERY OFFICE
BY HARRISON AND SONS, ST. MARTIN'S LANE,
PRINTERS IN ORDINARY TO HIS MAJESTY.

An additional measure taken to deal with the problem of boredom with bully beef was the issue of a tinned meat and vegetable ration based on roughly one of these rations two days a week. Opinions of the 'Maconochie' ration of meat and vegetables varied greatly and although some soldiers condemned them – one nickname was 'dog vomit' – George Coppard had this to say on the subject: 'Maconochie, a "dinner in a tin", was my favourite, and I could polish one with gusto, but the usual share-out was one tin for four men.'[85] By the spring of 1916 the meat ration had been adapted to consist of 60 per cent frozen meat, 25 per cent preserved meat, 15 per cent meat and vegetable rations and the same of pork and bean rations. All of the last three being tinned and ideal for issue to men in the trenches. One problem with the meat and vegetable ration was that it was regarded as being 'too rich and sickly', and the nature of the pork and bean ration was often commented upon in an unfavourable way. This was because the contents chiefly consisted of haricot beans to which pork fat was blended. The *Official History* suggests, somewhat after the fact, that it would have been better if this ration had been termed 'baked beans'. However, an interesting point is made that 'the full nutritive value of the pork and bean rations was not utilized as many men swallowed the beans without chewing them and they appeared unchanged in the faeces'.[86] One wonders which member of the RAMC conducted this field research and under what circumstances!

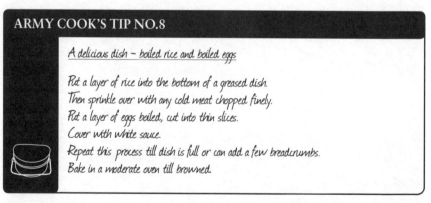

ARMY COOK'S TIP NO.8

A delicious dish – boiled rice and boiled eggs

Put a layer of rice into the bottom of a greased dish.
Then sprinkle over with any cold meat chopped finely.
Put a layer of eggs boiled, cut into thin slices.
Cover with white sauce.
Repeat this process till dish is full or can add a few breadcrumbs.
Bake in a moderate oven till browned.

From Log Book of G.N.R. Smith, 368 Siege Battery, RGA

For the majority of the journey, rations would be still packed in their crates and sacks to make movement easier and more convenient. Only at the point where rations needed to be divided up for sub units at platoon and section level, ten to thirty men, would it be necessary to open crates and count out tins, loaves or biscuits. One aspect of the tinned rations that resulted in comment was the fact that some ration tins were damaged in transit. This meant that the contents were putrid by the time they reached the men, although this could not be detected until the tin was opened in the conventional way. Troops solved the problem of detecting 'safe' and 'putrid' tins by the simple expedient of stabbing them with the marlinspike on the issue jack knife. The opinion was that if a tin 'fizzed' when pierced it was to be thrown away. Both bully beef and Maconochie are often condemned in soldiers' memoirs, and archaeological research carried out on the Western Front has demonstrated that, in addition to empty tins, a very large amount of full tins were abandoned by soldiers. Whether they were fed up with the weight or the taste is not clear.

The bread ration remained unchanged until early 1917, when attacks on allied shipping convoys meant that the amount of bread and biscuit was reduced and partially replaced by a ration of oatmeal and rice. Although the quality of biscuit improved as the war progressed it remained unpopular and the men preferred bread. This was unfortunate, as it was more difficult to get fresh bread to the frontline and it was frequently stale. Early in the war, it was recognised that loaves were difficult to ship and the expedient was the use of 'offal sacks', which were produced for the use of slaughterhouses to ship offal. It was found that a single sack could accommodate fifty 1½lb loaves. This was sufficient ration for 100 men. This meant that ten sacks would provide the full requirement for a battalion.[87] By the middle of the war the principal depots where bread was produced in bulk were Boulogne, Le Havre, Rouen, Dieppe and Calais. Each produced thousands of loaves and it was calculated that their combined output on any one day was 1,735,418lb of bread.[88]

ARMY COOK'S TIP NO.9

Stale Bread

1) It can be made equal to new baked bread by being immersed in cold water and rebaked for about one hour.

2) Slices or bits can be dipped in milk and baked in hot oven. This process makes delicious rusks which can be used in many ways.

From Log Book of G.N.R. Smith, 368 Siege Battery, RGA

George Coppard's view was that 'A bread ration was seldom seen … The hard biscuits which were issued must have been torture for men with false teeth, who had to soak them in water.'[89] The attention to detail that went into placing the contracts for the supply of such items as the biscuit is illuminating. According to 53/Gen. No./5399 and Contract B. 784 in the Handbook of Specifications for Supplies, 1915:

> The Biscuit is to be made of – (Whole wheat meal and pure wheat flower in the proportion of 3/8ths of the former to 5/8ths of the latter, the produce of good, sound, sweet, and dry wheat, without any adulterations whatever, and with the addition of not less than 4 per cent and not more than 5 per cent of pure sugar (sucrose). The biscuit should not contain more than 8 per cent of moisture, and no extraneous brand must be added.'

The contract goes on to specify how the biscuits are to be packed, in tinned steel boxes, with a 6in opening covered by a soldered disc. Below the opening 'shall be placed a card or paper with the description of the contents, the name of the contractor, and the date (month and year) of manufacture clearly printed on it'.[90] One wonders whether the attention to detail shown in placing the order might have been lost on men receiving the finished product?

Bacon was always a popular ration item, even though it could be very fatty. Butter and margarine were issued three times a week, although margarine became the norm as the war progressed. Cheese was popular, but the manner in which loose rations were conveyed could result in problems for the recipients. As Coppard indicates:

BISCUIT.

53/*Gen. No.*/5399 and *Contracts* B. 784.

1. The biscuit is to be made of—

(*a*) Whole wheat meal and pure wheat flour in the proportion of ⅜ths of the former to ⅝ths of the latter, the produce of good, sound, sweet, and dry wheat, without any adulteration whatever, and with the addition of not less than 4 per cent. and not more than 5 per cent. of pure sugar (sucrose). The biscuit should not contain more than 8 per cent. of moisture, and no extraneous bran must be added, OR,

(*b*) Pure wheat flour, the produce of good, sound, sweet, and dry wheat, without any adulteration whatever. The biscuit should contain no bran, and not more than 8 per cent. of moisture.

2. *Small Button Biscuit.*—The button biscuit to be either oval or square, and to be made from whole wheat meal and pure wheat flour, as in the case of biscuit referred to in paragraph 1 (*a*) and (*b*) above. The number of these biscuits to the pound will depend upon the dimensions of the cutters, but the pack required is for 200 to 240 biscuits to the pound, with 20 lbs. to each canister.

3. The biscuit meal and flour to be in all respects equal to samples approved by the O.C., Supply Reserve Depôt, Deptford Cattle Market, London, S.E.

4. The meal and flour to be subject to inspection by an officer deputed for the purpose at the place where the biscuit is made, not only in a dry state, but during any stage of manufacture, if desired.

5. The biscuit to be supplied closely packed by hand, so as to avoid movement during transit, in well made hermetically sealed tin canisters soldered throughout with resin (the solder used to contain not less than 50 per cent. of tin), 15 lbs. or 25 lbs. nett in each canister, as may be required.

6. The canisters to be made of selected 1.c. plates (*i.e.*, the weight of 112 sheets, 20 ins. × 14 ins., shall be 108 lbs.), best Siemens steel, coke finish, suitable for deep stamping, coated with pure tin in not less quantity than 2·5 lbs. (or an amount not falling anywhere below 0·0361 gramme to the square inch, both sides, to ensure a fair distribution of the tin), to 112 sheets; thoroughly cleaned before filling, and provided with a round countersunk air-tight lid in centre (6-inch opening) with discs tagger 7½ inches in diameter, made of light casket tin, with a sunk circle, ¾ of an inch from outer rim.

7. Immediately under the disc of each canister shall be placed a card or paper with description of the contents, the name of contractor, and the date (month and year) of manufacture clearly printed on it.

The words " To open—cut round sunk circle with penknife " to be stamped in half-inch letters in centre of disc.

8. The canisters to be packed in wooden service cases, made in accordance with War Department Specification.

9. The canisters and discs to be equal in all respects to the Standard patterns, which may be seen on application to the O.C., Supply Reserve Depôt, Deptford Cattle Market, London, S.E.

From 'Handbook of Specifications for Supplies, 1915'.

Approved, 18th March, 1916.

BUTTER.

1. The butter to be current season's butter, not renovated nor containing renovated butter, the genuine product of cow's milk, clean, well made, sound, unadulterated, of good flavour, and equal in all respects to the sample approved by the O.C., Supply Reserve Depôt, Deptford Cattle Market, London, S.E.

2. The butter not to contain more than 16 per cent. of water nor more than 3 per cent. salt, and if boric acid is used as a preservative the quantity must not exceed 0.5 per cent.

3. The butter to be open to inspection during the process of, and after manufacture and packing.

4. The butter will not be accepted if, on analysis, it is found to contain tin in excess of 2 grains per lb.

5. To be supplied in well-made hermetically sealed tins, the tops and bottoms to be spun on, or closed by the double-seaming process. Each tin to contain 1 lb. or 2 lbs. net of butter, and to be packed in wooden service cases, made in accordance with War Department specification, 40 1-lb. tins or 20 2-lb. tins to the case.

6. The tins to be made of selected 1.c.1. plates (*i.e.*, the weight of 112 sheets, 20 ins. × 14 ins., shall be 100 lbs.), best Siemens steel, coke finish, suitable for deep stamping, coated with pure tin in not less quantity than 2.5 lbs. (or an amount not falling anywhere below 0.0361 gramme to the square inch, both sides, to ensure a fair distribution of the tin) to 112 sheets, and thoroughly cleaned before filling. Each tin to have the date (month and year) of packing visibly stamped on it from the inside, thus—3.16. All the tins contained in a case to be the same date of canning.

The tins to be labelled with the description of the contents, the brand or name of the firm by whom the butter is prepared, and to be properly painted or lacquered all over (including that portion under the label) to preserve them from rust.

From 'Handbook of Specifications for Supplies, 1915'.

Wrapping loose rations such as tea, cheese and meat was not considered necessary, all being tipped into a sandbag, a ghastly mix-up resulting. In wet weather their condition was unbelievable, and you could bet that the rats would get at them first.[91]

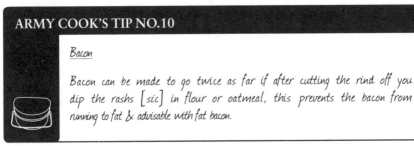

ARMY COOK'S TIP NO.10

Bacon

Bacon can be made to go twice as far if after cutting the rind off you dip the rashs [sic] in flour or oatmeal, this prevents the bacon from running to fat & advisable with fat bacon.

From Log Book of G.N.R. Smith, 368 Siege Battery, RGA

On the subject of jam, Coppard adds an immense amount of detail about the changing nature of this staple.

Tinned jam was an important part of our diet, and in the early days always seemed to be plum and apple, made by a firm named Tickler. It was not popular, and a derisory ditty went like this:

Tickler's jam, Tickler's jam,
How I love old Tickler's jam,
Plum and apple in a one pound pot,
Sent from blighty in a ten ton lot.
Every night when I'm asleep,
I'm dreaming that I am,
Forcing my way through the Dardanelles,
With a ton of Tickler's jam.

Soldier's jam took on a new look when Australia supplied such varieties as Quince Conserve, Melon and Honey and Pineapple. I do not recollect ever receiving an apple or an orange as part of my rations in France.[92]

From Log Book of G.N.R. Smith, 1917.

Rhubarb : Jam

Instead of making plain Rhubarb which does not keep very well use only the half quantity of rhubarb and substitute Figs for the other half

Less sugar is needed and the Jam is delicious

Good
G.N.R.S.

COMMANDANT
COMMAND SCHOOL OF COOKERY
MAY 1917
No.
ALDERSHOT.

If George Coppard did not receive an orange it was not because the Director General of Medical Services did not want him to have one. In the middle of the war it was suggested that, as the amount of fresh vegetables available for issue were declining well below the 8oz specified and dried vegetables were not an adequate substitute, an orange should be issued to each man daily.

VEGETABLES

The vegetables in common use by the troops are Potatoes, Carrots, Turnips, Onions, Beans, Vegetable Marrows, Turnip Tops, Greens and Cabbage.

From Log Book of Col P.R. Froud, Feb. 1917

Quite how nearly 2 million oranges a day, or 14 million a week, were to be transported to Flanders is another question! Proof that oranges were issued can be seen in the memoirs of a First Line Transport driver serving with an infantry battalion. In the spring of 1917, he recalls that:

> We got some peculiar ration issues about this time; sometime four dates per man would be given out in lieu of a butter issue. At others, we got about twenty raisins per man, only to learn that they were in place of our jam ... Other weird issues that made their appearance were five-sixths or two thirds of an orange per man and a handful of chestnuts.[93]

Quite why the official ration was a share of an orange may be explained by an experience from a few days later, which also shows why so many frontline soldiers were convinced that the ASC had the best rations:

> All the drivers engaged in drawing rations from the railhead – ASC and ourselves – were surreptitiously handed an orange and a box of matches each by the NCO in charge![94]

However, a veteran of the Great War indicated that oranges would not have been popular in the trenches, as it was impossible to wash – and toilet paper was in short supply – and men in his experience had a 'clean hand' and a 'dirty' one. As unpeeled apples could be eaten with one hand, they were popular. This could not be said for oranges.

ARMY COOK'S TIP NO.11

To prevent greens from boiling over, add a piece of fat about the size of a walnut.

From Log Book of G.N.R Smith, 368 Siege Battery, RGA

One feature of Great War rations, which is frequently mentioned, is the daily issue of rum and in particular its issue before an attack. As George Coppard comments in his memoir:

Rum proved to be a shock. At Givenchy I had my first issue of rum. It was not enough to get me mad and make me want to take on the whole German army, but it was jolly welcome for all that. It must have been proof spirit for its fire nearly choked me.[95]

Many soldiers of the time and the generation subsequently believed that the letters 'SRD' marked on the jars in which the rum was delivered stood for Seldom Reaches Destination or Service Rum Dilute. It actually stood for Supply Reserve Depot and was there to ensure that the 'empties' were returned to the depot in Woolwich for reuse. Sadly for the troops, the SRD jar could also contain lime juice or other issue liquids and although thousands of jars are still in circulation today, they are not all 'Rum Jars'. Even more unfortunate were men in units in which the commanding officer did not approve of the issue of alcohol. These men received pea soup in the form of concentrated blocks, 'Soup Squares', which were reconstituted with water by the cooks or the men themselves; being a 'Pea Souper' was not popular. It must be clear that, as George Coppard has already indicated, the official issue of rum would not be sufficient to get a man fighting drunk, and as the issue had to be consumed at the time of issue there was no opportunity to hoard alcohol for a future binge.

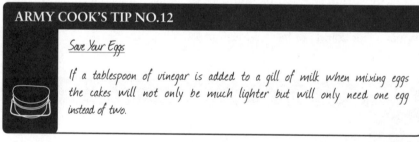

ARMY COOK'S TIP NO.12

Save Your Eggs

If a tablespoon of vinegar is added to a gill of milk when mixing eggs the cakes will not only be much lighter but will only need one egg instead of two.

From Log Book of G.N.R. Smith, 368 Siege Battery, RGA

Tobacco was also issued as a regular ration, but like other items that were rather desirable this was sometimes in short supply. According to George Coppard: 'Weekly rations usually included twenty, perhaps thirty, cigarettes per man but most Tommies relied on parcels from home for their main supplies'.[96] He confirms the importance of cigarettes and states:

'cigarettes were as important as ammunition. A Tommy would ask for a fag when near death, as if it was some kind of opiate that relieved pain and smoothed the path to oblivion'.[97]

Another aspect of the Great War which has attracted critical attention, is the better rations received by officers compared to the men; in reality the ration scale for officers was identical to that of the Other Ranks. They did, however, have the advantage of a 'Soldier Servant', known incorrectly by some as a 'Bat Man'. (The term Bat Men came from the British Army in India as transport horses were 'Bat' horses and were specifically used for transporting an officer's kit.) If an officer's rations were better than the men's it was because he had privately purchased the food or had it sent to him. Private Beatson was the beneficiary of an officer's hospitality:

Sellers and I had to wait in a dug-out on orders and we had a pleasant chat and a glorious tuck-in with Lieutenant Robb who had just returned from hospital and brought a delicious gingerbread cake with him. We made oxo and tea on a little Pocket Primer he carries. [98]

On another occasion the officer may not have been so aware of his generosity:

Had a fine spread with Lance Corporal Watson from the officer's serv- ants at Headquarters yesterday. The Colonel's cook produced a second course of custard, stewed rhubarb and milk – tres bon.[99]

Even a private could receive a parcel from home or do some extra shop- ping, and when behind the lines, Beatson comments that: 'It was against the grain to do 2½ hours drill but our "al fresco" dinner made up for it. Melton Mowbray pie, pineapple, cake, dates and chocolate sitting on a blanket in the sun'.[100] One wonders whether the less fortunate members of the unit received the benefits of the 'no show' by some of the men for whom rations had been prepared by the cooks?

Hospitals and convalescent camps in Britain and closer to the front had their own ration scales. These were intended to help the recovery of the wounded without overfeeding, whilst at the same time appealing to the appetite of men confined to a hospital ward or camp. Olive Dent, a VAD (Volunteer Aid Detachment) working in hospitals in France, described the cooking arrangements:

I looked round, for the kitchens were beautiful – spotlessly clean, exquisitely tidy and admirably well-ordered, though at the time, some thousands of dinners were being prepared ... The dinner which was being cooked consisted of a most deliciously smelling stew made from the Army ration of mixed vegetables and meat, supplemented with fresh onions, carrots and suet dumplings.[101]

A further description of the meals gives an indication of what could be achieved, even though she makes the point that female cooks could have done a more economical job than the male cooks she encountered:

The breakfast each morning had consisted of tea, bread, fried bacon, boiled bacon or boiled ham, and on two mornings of the week, potted meat, and on a third, rissoles in additions ... Tea each day had consisted of tea, bread, cheese and butter, or cheese and jam, with Saturday's and Sunday's meal augmented with potted meat. Supper consisted of soup with bread or biscuit, of butter, cheese and biscuits of bread, with tea or cocoa.[102]

ARMY COOK'S TIP NO.13

When making a boiled suet pudding if equal quantities of stale bread soaked in cold water and squeezed dry in a cloth and flour is used — it is far superior to one made with all flour.

From Log Book of G.N.R. Smith, 368 Siege Battery, RGA

Miss Dent's experience of cookery for the wounded can be compared with that of one private soldier who, while recovering from his injury, was sent to No.6 Convalescent Camp. According to his account, his meals were badly prepared and inadequate:

For Breakfast: One slice of bread and jam and a knob of cheese. For Dinner: Bully and machonachie [sic], followed by a filthy concoction of soppy biscuits and dates. For Tea: One slice of bread and jam.[103]

One wonders if this critical assessment of food in a convalescent camp indicates that at least some of the troops were content with the rations they received in training and the frontline. The main criticism he gives is that the rations are little better than field rations, with none of the fresh ingredients that he might have expected. It must be remembered that both in Britain and on the continent individual camps contracted with local suppliers for fresh food to supplement rations. This, of course, also reduced the amount of stores shipped to Britain and France, in addition to cutting the level of railway traffic. This represented a considerable saving of space, which could be used for items not available through local purchase, such as ammunition.

The author interviewed a veteran of the Great War who served in the Guernsey Light Infantry. Whilst recovering in hospital from wounds he received in action, a member of the hospital came into the ward and asked if there were any French speakers among the patients. As he had grown up on Guernsey, he was bi-lingual and was able to demonstrate this in a conversation with a farmer who had come to the hospital kitchen to sell produce. This went well and, on his recovery, he was given the task of being the hospital interpreter, largely bartering with local tradesmen and farmers. He was so successful that he was not returned to his unit for some months. As he marched up to the front with a draft of reinforcements they were stopped by an officer and told that with effect from 11 o'clock that day the war had ended. He always felt that his command of French might have saved his life.

FROM THE MESS TIN
TO THE MESS HALL

THE 1910 MANUAL of Military Cooking states that 'to cook rapidly and well is an art which can be easily acquired, and which every soldier should learn'.[104] When the manual was written Britain was at peace and if war was envisaged it was seen in terms of a brief mobile campaign that would be over 'before Christmas'. What followed, in 1914, was a brief period of manoeuvre warfare followed by trench stalemate. The circumstances the British Army faced were new, and the means of cooking had to be adapted to the nature of trench warfare. No planning had taken place for the conditions in which the men now found themselves living, and it makes sense to consider cookery in the Great War from the various situations that existed during the conflict. As the 1918 Manual of Military Cooking and Dietary makes clear, 'circumstances vary considerably in the several stations'. In the manual, Part 1 is intended for use in 'home stations', and Part 2 in 'the field'.[105]

ARMY COOK'S TIP NO.14

When using yeast don't add too much salt as it hinders the action of the yeast.

From Log Book of G.N.R. Smith, 368 Siege Battery, RGA

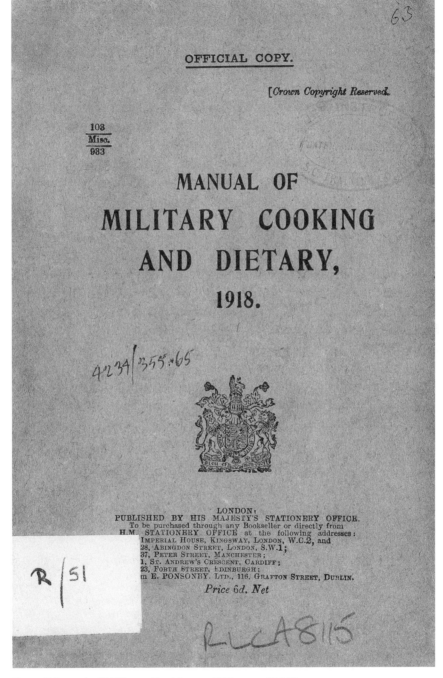

OFFICIAL COPY.

[Crown Copyright Reserved.

103
Miso.
983

MANUAL OF
MILITARY COOKING
AND DIETARY,
1918.

LONDON:
PUBLISHED BY HIS MAJESTY'S STATIONERY OFFICE.
To be purchased through any Bookseller or directly from
H.M. STATIONERY OFFICE at the following addresses:
IMPERIAL HOUSE, KINGSWAY, LONDON, W.C.2, and
28, ABINGDON STREET, LONDON, S.W.1;
37, PETER STREET, MANCHESTER;
1, ST. ANDREW'S CRESCENT, CARDIFF;
23, FORTH STREET, EDINBURGH;
m E. PONSONBY. LTD., 116, GRAFTON STREET, DUBLIN.

Price 6d. Net

From 'Manual of Military Cooking and Dietary, 1918'.

To better understand how cooking was tackled in the 'several stations' we will start 'in the field', specifically in the trenches. One has to refer back to 1910 Manual of Military Cooking to find a specific recommendation concerning the most basic form of cookery: that in the soldier's individual mess tin.[106]

It was during the Peninsula War that British soldiers first received an issue individual cooking vessel called, not surprisingly, the 'mess tin'. This was a two-part tin-plated steel item, roughly D-shaped, to fit against the body or pack, for the infantry and circular for mounted troops. It was provided with a handle so it could be held over a fire or used as an eating vessel. It was far from ideal as too much heat would cause the tin plate to melt and they were difficult to keep clean. The circumstances when mess tins were used for cookery were chiefly when men were in the trenches or on the march. At other times, they served as the principal container for cooked meals when they were issued, and the lid made a convenient receptacle for tea or other drinks. Although there was training in mess tin cookery, it was the responsibility of each man to ensure that he was competent as his own cook. The 1910 Manual contains the following simple advice:

> A mess tin will cook one man's meat with vegetables and two men's without ... Small fires only are required, as rapid boiling makes meat tough and hard. If possible grease the tins on the outside before placing them on a fire; this makes them easier to clean afterwards.

Mess Tin Recipe No.1
Baking Powder Loaf Tin

Ingredients:

Flour,	a Pinch Salt,
Baking Powder,	Water

Method of Preparation:

- Mix flour, salt & baking powder in mess tin lid being careful there are no lumps left in baking powder. Make a bay in the centre, pour in water.
- Mix into a stiff dough.
- Then put on a floured board and work into a round.
- Cut both ways across the centre so as to resemble a Coburg shape loaf.
- Grease mess tin on the outside.
- Put loaf in and lid on.
- Then put to bake, being careful not to have too much fire underneath, most on top.
- Time to cook about 20 minutes.

From Exercise Book of Pte A.E. Purssell, No. 39246

The fact that all mess tins were issued with a linen cover indicates that whatever cleaning they received they would be frequently distinctly 'grubby' after use. In some circumstances, it was possible to economise on fuel by piling up mess tens around a single fire, although the manual makes it clear 'that no more than 10 tins should be placed around one fire'.[107] The 1910 Manual also suggests that dinners of 'Plain Stew, Irish stew, curried stew, Sea Pies and Meat Puddings' can be prepared using this method of cooking in between '1 hour to 1½ hours'.[108]

Mess Tin Recipe No.2
Chappatis

Ingredients:

Flour,	Salt,	Water

Method of Preparation:

• Mix flour and salt in mess tin lid. Make a bay in centre, pour water in.
• Mix into a medium stiff dough.
• Bring out on a floured board.
• Roll out the size of the mess tin lid.
• Put a little salt in mess tin lid and hold over the fire a minute or so.
• Then put the dough in and bake of fry until it becomes a golden brown.
• The salt will prevent sticking.

From Exercise Book of Pte A.E. Purssell, No. 39246

Whether these rations could be prepared adequately depended upon the skill of the cook. The memoirs of an un-named private in the 56th (London) Division explains the outcome of his first effort to cook for a small mess:

After my first attempt at cooking they one and all declared I should never be allowed to touch the Primus stove again, so now I enjoy the luxury of eating boiled custard or tapioca, etc., without helping to make it. The reason is simple. I tried to fry six eggs, smashed one and served up the five as a yellow mess covering the bottom of the frying pan; following this by a terrible concoction made of salt and flour in mistake for sugar and custard-powder.[109]

MESS TIN COOKING

The mess tins should be placed on the ground, the oval part of the tin on the outside with the opening facing the direction of the wind. 8 is a convenient number of tins to form a kitchen, but 3 to 11 can be used. The handles of the tins should be placed on the outside before being placed on the fire, if this is done and they are cleaned soon afterwards they will suffer no damage to the tins and when they are hot they can be cleaned in a few minutes with turf, soil or hay.

Only a small quantity of wood is required for each kitchen and food weight being the object to keep in view. The fuel should be obtained near the kitchen, when mess tins are used every man should be instructed to prepare his own food, but when in the kitchen one man need only remain with each fire. The position of tins require to be changed occasionally. The dinners can be cooked in 1½ hours from the time of placing on the fire. Suitable dishes for mess tin cooking are Plain Stew, Irish Stew, Sea Pie, Curried Stew, Meat Puddings.

BRAZIER FOR MESS TINS.

Brazier for mess tins. From 'Manual of Military Cooking and Dietary, 1918'.

The big danger in frontline cookery was the telltale smoke, and the ability to cook a meal or even heat water for a 'brew' became an art form. In the early months of the war, the only means of heating food in the trenches was braziers, which were regarded as being 'neither satisfactory nor sufficient'.[110] Some soldiers bought, or received from home, a primus stove or a device called the 'Tommy Cooker'. This was a tin containing a gel not unlike modern firelighters, that could be used to heat a cup of tea or tin of stew. These became an issue item once their value had been established, but they continued to be in short supply. Once the user had finished, the lid could be replaced, snuffing out the flames and preserving the remaining fuel for future use. If a soldier was not fortunate enough to have access to a Tommy Cooker or had run out of fuel, improvising was the order of the day. One example of this is the use of strips of sandbags soaked in melted candle wax or tiny chips of wood that burnt quickly and were, in theory, smokeless. Another was using a galvanised bucket or old petrol tin with punctured sides as an improvised stove. These could be used by a number of soldiers but needed an alarming amount of coke or charcoal. Some men were keen to avoid anything that might leave them without the means to produce a hot drink in the line.

Private Kenneth Garry, an infantryman in the Honourable Artillery Company, recalled that he ensured that, in addition to the usual full set of equipment, he carried 'my pocket primus, and a tin of paraffin, two small tins of Heinz baked beans ... a Tommy's cooker and a tin of re-fill'.[111]

To improve the quality of cookery and quantity of meals provided, cooks were gradually moved closer to the frontline as the war progressed. In November 1916 Private Dolden recalled:

This time we took over 'B' Company's old positions in the frontline trench. There were two cookhouses, one of which was in the frontline itself, with the comforting feeling that the Germans were very close and practically neighbours ...

The neighbours were not always friendly and in 1917, in a similar position close to the lines, the cooks over did things in their haste to prepare rations: 'We made a tremendous coal fire in the cookhouse. There was such a reek of smoke that everybody "got the wind up". An Officer came along and ordered us to reduce smoke'.[112] By 1918 he was able to report

Mess tin cooking: this recreation uses original rations and mess tins to demonstrate how a soldier would have provided for himself while in a frontline trench. Note the 'popular' Machonocie ration tin.

Tea was frequently made using a Tommy Cooker, embedded in the trench wall. Tea was a luxury, so grains had to be measured out carefully.

A strip of sandbag soaked in candle wax was often enough to start a fire, lighting as soon as a match was applied, but often fires were also built up with kindling. Saving fuel was key, and ensuring that the fire would heat up quickly and be as smokeless as possible were important skills for the Tommy cook to master.

The cooking vessel would be suspended or propped over the flames, held in place by the trench walls. An army cook was never to leave the fire unattended.

Despite a cook's best efforts it was almost impossible to stop smoke escaping over the trench parapet and giving off tell-tale signs of occupation to the enemy on the other side of no man's land.

A Soyer Stove showing the tinned inner boiler.

Building an Aldershot Oven.

The Aldershot Oven in use. First, the oven must be fired through, with the fire building an intense heat within the brick base and metal walls, which is retained after the fire dies down. This is obviously not a smoke-free process!

that 'a portion of a dugout was set aside for us, but we were only allowed to cook at night, since it was the first occasion on which cooking had ever been done in that part of the line, and the Battalion did not want to advertise the fact to the enemy...'[113]

This was an unusual solution to the problem of providing hot meals and, more usually, the meals were prepared behind the lines and sent forward by carrying parties at night. To keep the food hot, the use of 'pan-packs', or 'hay boxes', and other improvised insulated containers in which food could be taken to the trenches while it was still cooking was successfully developed. The rations were cooked in dixies, as usual, but shortly before the process was finished the container was placed into a box filled with hay. This insulation kept the food warm and in most conditions the food or tea would remain warm for considerable time in the hay box. It was estimated that the food could be kept at temperature up to eighteen hours. By 1917, a purpose-made container for food or hot liquids was being produced and is described by the cook Private Dolden.

> We made meals as usual, and these were carried up to the boys in iron containers. These were lined with asbestos to keep the heat in, and were slung with straps on the back of the carrier.[114]

Another form of carrier was the use of 2 gallon petrol tins insulated with felt and waterproof fabric in which hot drinks such as cocoa could be carried up to the trenches. The official history of the RAMC specifies that distribution of hot drinks was especially important between 2 and 4 a.m.[115] As Private Coppard's experience shows units even went so far as to provide special soup kitchens at brigade level which were located near 'gum boot', Wellington boot, stores, so that men proceeding to or returning from the trenches could receive dry foot wear and a hot drink.[116] All of these arrangements demonstrate the sophistication that was eventually achieved in the distribution of appropriate rations for men on the Western Front.

Although an improvised kitchen could be prepared on the front or support lines, the most usual way of cooking meals for infantry units was a pre-war innovation. Every infantry company, roughly 200 men, was provided with a Travelling Kitchen. This horse-drawn vehicle consisted of two parts. The first was the limber in which stores and tools could be kept, and

HAY BOX.

The Hay Box will keep food hot for a considerable time. Certain food will continue to cook if put in the Hay Box at boiling point. It will not cook pastry which requires the top heat of an oven, or pudding which requires the contents of a cooking vessel to be kept at boiling point. It will not cook cabbage or certain vegetables which should boil rapidly. There is a great saving of fuel and the Hay Box should invariably be used when cooking for small Units, Detachments, Guards, Piquets, etc. A pad made of hay should be placed on top of the cooking vessel before closing the lid.

Hay box. From 'Manual of Military Cooking and Dietary, 1918'.

the other the main body or cooker. This was fitted with a chimney and could be used as a stationary cooker or to keep the food warm, even when on the march. The cooker was fitted with four boilers for cooking meals and a central 8 gallon boiler with a tap, in which water or stock could be stored without any chance of spillage. The limber housed a further four boilers, giving a total capacity of more than 58 gallons.[117] It was also possible to remove several of the frying pans and cooking vessels so that cooking could be conducted over a trench fire if required. A number of dixies were carried on the limber so meals could be sent to men who were in frontline or other positions. Only the simplest meal could be produced from the travelling kitchen, the type of cooking being limited to boiling and frying. The Manual of Military Cooking, 1918 estimates that a meal could be prepared within one hour of lighting the fire in the cooker.[118]

TRAVELLING KITCHEN

The travelling kitchen consists of 2 parts, body and limber. The limber consists of 4 asbestos lined chambers in which to place the tanks from the
body as their contents are cooked for the purpose of keeping them hot.
The chambers will keep food almost at boiling point for 8 hours, it will keep
them warm for 24 hours. The limber also contains 1 cupboard. The door of
which when opened will lay flat forming a cutting up or preparing board. In
the top of the cupboard are fitted 4 pull out **bowls** as follows: 2 for sugar, 1
for tea, 1 wood lined for salt. 2 iron lockers are fixed under limber in rear of
axle and open under cupboard. 4 frying pans are supplied and are strapped
2 on each side of the limber, they are made to fit in place of tanks on
the body when required for frying purposes, 2 grease boxes are strapped
under cupboard one each side, one **basher** wallet is strapped on front
of limber, cupboard and locker are the only places in which to keep stores
and utensils, the locker for small utensils. The whole of this is mounted on 2
wheels and concreted to the body by a trail hook and eye.

Body of cooker consists of 4 tanks or Boiler holes for cooking food
and 1 Tank fitted with a tap which is for water, and is only taken out
for cleaning pruposes. 8 Tanks or boilers are supplied each with splash
plates and lids and are inter-changeable and each has a capacity of 5 gallons. The tap tank also holds 5 gallons. The fire box is in rear of cooker
and the stock pipe in the centre. There are 2 fuel boxes, one on each
side of fire box, 1 lifting rod is fitted on rear side of cooker. Cooking
capacity for 252 men. Weight 37 ¼ **cuts** when loaded with 262 men's
rations for 24 hours. The body is fixed on 2 wheels and connected to
limber by a large hook, 1 iron rake is fitted either side of body, a brake
is fitted on both sides, struts are provided which when bit down allow
both limber and body to stand rigid.

Consumption of fuel for 150 men's dinners, consisting of Sea Pie, Haricot
Beans, Boiled Ham, Boiled Meat, Figs & Custard – fuel used 30 to 40lb.
Utensils: 2 Hand bowls, 1 Butcher's cleaver, 1 Butcher's saw, 1 Canvas
holdall in locker, 6 Butcher's knives, 2 Steels, 6 Tin openers, 1 Felling axe,
1 Slade, 1 Pickaxe, 1 Rifle rack, 1 Blanket for horse, 2 dixies on front for
officer's use.

Units such as the RAMC, artillery and other corps' troops had to make do with the traditional Soyer Stove. They regretted bitterly that they did not get the advantage that the Field Kitchens provided, as it took time to set up the stoves and prepare a hot meal or drink. The Soyer Stove was an innovation that dated to the Crimean War, 1854–56. It was invented by the French Chef Alexis Soyer as an economical and efficient way to cook for groups of soldiers in virtually any conditions. The stove was made of steel and was cylindrical and it stood on short legs. Under the lid was a tinned steel cooking vessel which contained up to 12 gallons and below that the fire, fed through a small hatch in the front centre, the chimney rising up from the back. It was estimated that the stove could provide vegetables or puddings for fifty men and far more rations in the form of soup or hot drinks. The inventor had refused to patent it in case anyone would think that his offer of the 'Soyer Stove' to the army had been made for his personal profit.[119] The great advantage of the Soyer Stove was the economical way in which it used fuel, was light and portable and could be used without the flame being seen. The stove could be used for stews, stocks and soups plus making tea, coffee and hot chocolate. Its adaptability was a great asset and an enormous advantage over previous systems of open fire cookery. As the heating chamber was separated from the cooking vessel there could be great variety in the fuel used. The stove worked well with timber, coke or coal, turf or peat and in emergency dried camel dung could be burned; no doubt this added a little flavouring to soups and stews. Soyer Stoves could be grouped together to form a kitchen for a unit and each stove could be used for a different purpose. In combination with improvised cookers called, at the time, Camp Kettle or Dixie Trench, and similar forms of improvised ovens a wide variety of meals could be prepared. The limitation was always the knowledge and ingenuity of the cooks and the availability of fuel and ingredients. The 1910 Manual provides four pages of instruction on how meals can be prepared in the field in the absence of a travelling kitchen.[120]

The field kitchen could be simple or elaborate, depending upon how long the unit was likely to be in one place, but took the form of a series of trenches, either dug down into the ground or built up with stones or bricks facing, or possibly across, the prevailing wind direction. The unit camp kettles could then be heated from underneath by fires built in the trenches with a flow of heat running under a number of kettles at once.

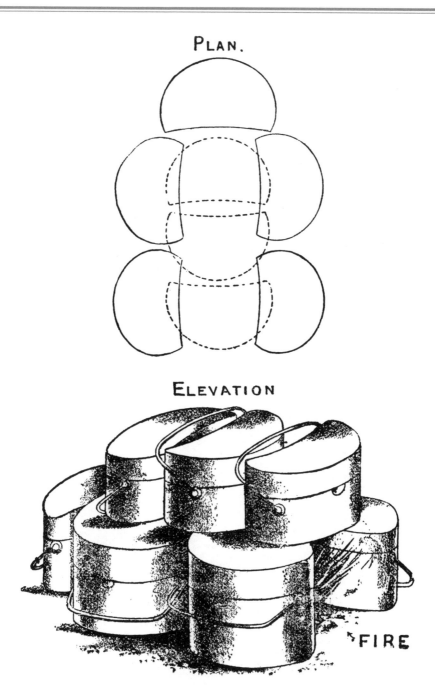

PLAN.

ELEVATION

FIRE

Diagram of how to arrange kettle drums over a single fire. From 'Manual of Military Cooking and Dietary, 1918'.

Ques

Ans

What does the hardtired Field Ration consist of

14 ozs of bread   2 ozs of Bacon
12 " " Meat   1/2 " Tea   5 1/2 in each
2 " " Sugar   1/4 " Salt   per man per day
10 1/2 ozs of Flour can be drawn in lieu of Bread

Ques

How does a cook obtain his fung.

Ans

By the sale of by-products (not including swill)

11/- realized for 100 men in mess entitles a cook to obtain 6 per day
9/- realized entitles him to 3 per day
less than 9/- he gets nothing

Ques

Ans

When do you get bacon

Every other morning

Ques

Ans

How much stuffing should eat ration produce

At least 1/2 an oz

Ques

Ans

What are by products used for

1st Glass stuffing. Probly. Bones in lieu of Margarine

All other stuffing is sold for the extraction of glycerine which is turned into nitro glycerine for high explosive shells

Bones Invalua Stuff for agricultural purposes

Ques

Ans

How much meat is saved daily on each ration

About 2 ozs which provide rissoles sausages eac for breakfast

Ques

Ans

What are the chief duties of a cook

Cleanliness Economy Punctuality Simmer Skim Scour System

From Log Book of Cpl P.R. Froud, 1917.

The 1910 Manual suggests that 'Troops should have their dinners an hour and a half after rations are issued'.[121] If the unit was to be in one place for more than two days, an elaborate field kitchen, termed the 'Aldershot Grid Iron' Kitchen, based on a series of trenches leading to an improvised chimney could be constructed.[122] According to the manual, even when the simple form of kitchen is used it should be possible to have water boiling within 35 minutes of starting construction! An interesting suggestion is that the water used to boil potatoes should not be thrown away as it 'is required for washing-up'.[123] A host of differing forms of the kettle trench were advocated, ranging from the most basic to complicated semi-permanent structures built of brick and incorporating a range of oven, boilers and hot plates. All these required was raw materials and ingenuity.

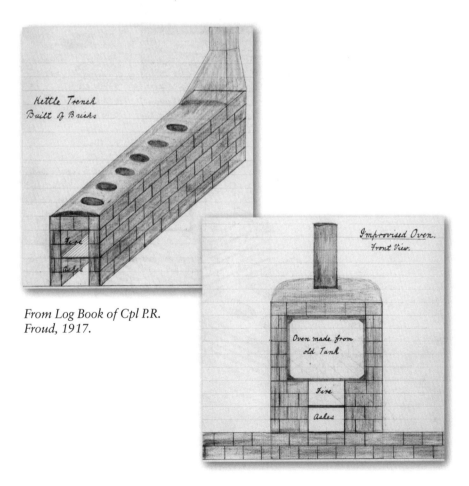

From Log Book of Cpl P.R. Froud, 1917.

103

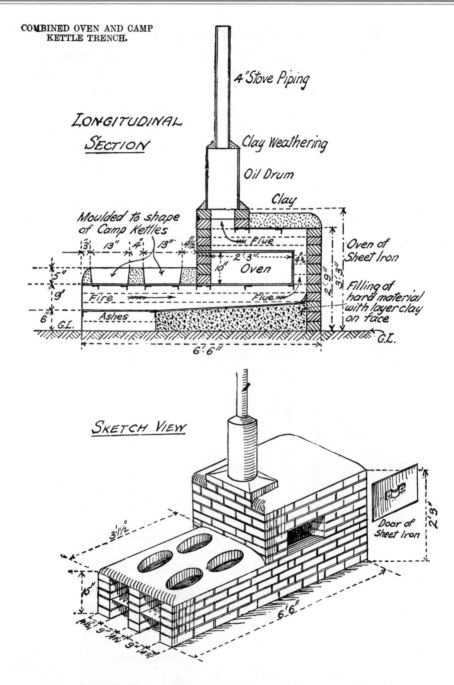

Combined oven and camp kettle trench. From 'Manual of Military Cooking and Dietary, 1918'.

KETTLE TRENCH FOR 150 MEN.

Construction of Kettle Trench.

Camp Kettle or Dixie Trenches can be constructed with bricks or tea or biscuit tins filled with mud. Build with bricks or lay the tins in two rows 9 or 10 inches apart, joining well together with clay, and put one tin at the end. Cover to a depth of 1 tin only from the mouth of the trench with a well perforated sheet of iron and lay on a second row of tins as before, cutting the front out of the tin to be placed at the end. Cover the whole length with another sheet of iron, having previously cut out the holes to fit the dixies, or lap strips of iron across as supports. Place the dixies in position, and cover well round with clay, sloping off slightly towards the sides to let the rain run off. Fit a chimney into the tin at the end, and cover well round with clay. The bed of the trench should slope gradually towards the chimney. The fire is only required at the mouth, and should not extend beyond the depth of one tin.

Kettle trench for 100 men. From 'Manual of Military Cooking and Dietary, 1918'.

MANAGEMENT OF FIELD KITCHENS

The management should be carried out in a similar manner to that in barracks, having a system for arranging every detail, seeing all orders are carried out after the necessary instructions have been given, keeping the ground clean both inside and outside of the kitchen.

For instance the wood should be chopped ready for use and kept in dry place. If using the watercart for the supply of water it should be placed in a position so that the water that drips from the cart runs away from the kitchen sewer, near the ovens or trenches.

The refuse tubs should be in such a position that the wind carries away any nasty smells from the kitchen. The cook pits should also be kept under strict observation allowing only the cooks to use it. All embers taken from the ovens and trenches should be placed in one heap so that they can easily be carted away.

The kitchen should be kept clean at all times, and a good supply of hot water kept for washing purposes. No dirty cooking vessels of any description should be allowed to remain dirty but washed up and returned to store, all utensils immediately after use should be washed up in soda water and put away in their proper places until required again. Great care should be paid to the refuse tubs, they should be emptied at least once a day and washed out with hot soda water and whitewashed on the outside. All meals should be served up at the appointed time, care being taken that they are kept as hot as possible. All meals should be laid out in their respective places so that they can be taken away quickly and quietly by the orderly men.

Great care should be paid to the ovens when cracks appear they should be properly plugged up and covered up at night in case of rain.

Trenches should be made so that rain can easily run away. The kettle trench should be made good whenever necessary. The day's work should never be considered finished until everything has been left in readiness for the next morning. The Sergt should make out a detail sheet every Saturday stating the duties of each company's cooks such as preparing party, cooking party & orderly cooks.

From Log Book of Cpl P.R. Froud, Feb. 1917

One item of issue equipment that, like the Soyer Stove and Field Cooker, could be used on active service was the 'Aldershot Oven'. Made of a curved wall and straight steel ends, the Aldershot Oven was heavy, at over 374lb (170kg), but it provided for great variations in styles of cookery. These metal components and issue tools could be transported easily on wagons, but were not suitable for the frontline. The metal components could not be used on their own and casing of up to 100 bricks, plus clay mixed with hay or straw to form 'pug', was required to encase the metal arch which sat on the issue bottom plate or a bed of bricks or hard clay. In its simplest form, it operated very much like a pizza oven, in which a fire was lit in the interior and allowed to burn for some time. This heated the metal plates that formed the roof and walls of the oven and the bricks and pug retained the heat so that it could be radiated back over a long cooking period. This meant that the oven temperature could be adjusted to allow the cook to prepare roast meats, pies or even Yorkshire puddings. One feature of the oven was that, as the pug dried out the subsequent firings used progressively less fuel. This meant that it was more economical in terms of both labour and fuel to leave an Aldershot Oven in a fixed position rather than move it too frequently. Heating on the first day would take up to four hours and 300lb of wood, compared to 1½ hours and 150lb of wood on the second heating.[124]

ALDERSHOT OVEN

An Aldershot Oven is built with a iron frame, turf and hay. The use of the oven is to cook meals for the troops when in the field it will bake meat, and potatoes, meat pies, cakes, jam, tarts, etc also bread. The oven consists of 2 sections, 2 ends, 1 bottom, 4 bars, 9 tins, 1 peel. If possible select a piece of ground on a gentle slope avoiding if possible all sandy or marshy ground, clay ground being the most suitable, prepare the sight [site], then place the bars on the arches, place the arches into position with the back overlapping the front fastening, the rings on top securely with wire then place the back end into position and fix securely with a iron stake and wire the back rings and handle of back end securely. Then place the front end into position to prevent the front of arch bending in, then build two rows of bricks and the mouth of oven, if bricks are not available tin cans filled with earth, or cut sods of earth or turf can be utilised. The clay or earth is then mixed and thrown over body of oven until a thickness of 12 inches at the front sloping to 9 inches at the back is obtained, carrying the slope to about 2 feet beyond the back of oven. The slope being made to carry off the rain and should be finished off gradually and neatly at back of oven. The oven when finished should be thoroughly dried, and any cracks that occur on top should be filled up with sand or dry clay. The bottom plate can be dispensed with and bottom of oven bricked (which is preferable). As it lasts much longer and bottom plate can be utilised as a hot plate.

From Log Book of Col P.R. Froud, Feb. 1917

The oven will bake 54.
2 or 2½ lb. loaves (108 rations)
and will cook dinners for 220.

Aldershot Oven.
2 arches.
2 Ends.
1. Bottom.
4. Bars.
9. Tins.
1. Peel.
Total Weight 374 lbs
3/4 cwt
Bottom 66 lbs

From Log Book of Cpl P.R. Froud, 1917.

After the allotted time for heating the oven was over, the bulk of the embers were drawn out with a rake, and any remaining ash was left as an even layer on the floor of the oven. At the beginning of the war the Aldershot Oven was used extensively for the baking of bread in France, but as the war progressed a number of patented steam bread ovens were installed in base depots, and the amount of baking in the Aldershot Oven was greatly reduced. In Britain, bread was initially supplied by civilian contractors, but as the war progressed twenty-two War Department bakeries were established, each with an average output of 50,000lb of bread per day.[125]

Dishes	Wood Required	Time. Table for Cooking Time for Heating
Baked Meat & Potatoes	180 lbs.	2 hours.
Meat. Pies	160 lbs.	2 hours.
Brown Stew.	150 lbs.	2 hours.
Fried Bacon.	90 to 100 lbs.	1 hour.
Fried Eggs.	90 to 100 lbs.	1 hour.
Soused Herrings	120 lbs.	1½ hours.
Fried Sausage.	100 lb.	1 hour.
Fried Rissoles	110 lbs.	1 hour.
Fried Liver.	120 lbs.	1½ hours.
Chops & Steaks.	130 lb.	1½ hours.
Milk Puddings	120 lb.	1½ hours.
Fruit Tarts.	110 lb.	1½ hours.
Jam Tarts	100 lb.	1½ hours.
Yorkshire Pudding.	110 lb.	1½ hours.

From Log Book of Cpl P.R. Froud, 1917.

an Aldershot Oven.

...ne for Cooking	If to be Lapped up	Remarks.
2½ Hours.	Yes.	Stock to cover Bottom.
2½ Hours.	Yes.	Grease Paper on Top.
2½ Hours.	Yes.	Barely Cover with Stock.
20 Minutes.	No.	1 Layer only.
5 Minutes.	No.	Fat covers Bottom of dish.
...0 Minutes.	No.	25 to 30 in each dish
...0 Minutes.	No.	one Layer only.
...0 Minutes.	No.	" " "
...6 Minutes.	No.	" " "
...0 Minutes.	No.	Frequently Charge.
...0 Minutes	No.	" "
...0 Minutes.	No.	" "
...7 Minutes.	No.	" "
...5 Minutes.	No.	" "

MANAGEMENT OF ALDERSHOT OVEN

It is essential that the oven should be thoroughly dry before any attempt is made to cook in it, no exact time is laid down for the drying of the oven as it depends upon the weather and the mixture used, but it usually takes about 3 days, only a small fire is necessary for this purpose about 200lb of wood a day being used, during the process of drying cracks will appear all over the oven these should not be filled up until all the steam has ceased to issue from them, this is important as it is the only way to tell if the oven is dry or otherwise.

Every night wood should be laid in the oven ready for lighting in the morning, it is thus kept dry. After lighting fire and bringing to required heat, the fire should be drawn and the embers swept clear with a broom which shall be dipped in water to prevent it getting burnt.

Dinners should then be placed in, the door quickly placed up, propped and plugged securely. If having a mixed diet of Baked Meat, Pies, Stews, etc the baked should be placed at the back, Pies in the centre and Stews in the front, then it will be found that they will all be done nicely at the same time.

Total weight of oven about 374lb. Length of oven when up 5ft 1in, width 3ft 6in (without covering) it will bake 54 2 or 2 ½ lb loaves (108 rations) or will cook dinner for about 220 men.

From Log Book of Col P.R. Froud, Feb. 1917

As it was not possible to control the oven temperature, other than by the amount of fuel used, and was impossible to measure accurately, a simple test was developed by which a cook could estimate how hot the oven temperature had become. The cook simply held the back of his bare hand towards the open door of the open and fired oven. If it was impossible to hold the hand in position for more than 5 seconds the oven was ready for meat and potatoes, 10 seconds brown stew and 14 seconds fruit pies.

If the metal components of the Aldershot Oven were not available, other improvised techniques were available to cooks. These included using hollowed out ant hills in tropical regions, using metal boxes full of earth or clay for walls or even using a barrel as a former over which damp clay could be shaped. Once the oven was fired the wooden elements of the barrel would burn away, leaving a void to act as an oven in future firings.[126]

On 'home station' permanent kitchens or cookhouses in unit depots were used, or were established, in the vast number of new training camps that sprang up after 1914. Although some of the initial camps were based on tents, more permanent huts soon replaced canvas and the arrival of piped water improved conditions for the cooks as much as for the men in training. Troops in training or on exercise sometimes found themselves away from the cookhouse, in circumstances where they would have to cook for themselves. Early in his training, a private soldier of the London Rifle Brigade (LRB) was given the task of preparing breakfast for his unit in a school playground. His first mistake was being unable to light a fire and his second was leaving the kitchen unattended when he went in search of fuel. On his return he discovered that men from the Highland Light Infantry (HLI) had 'acquired' his small stock:

> On my return the light from the neighboring fire doubtless reflected the misery upon my face. There was no doubt where our fuel had go to: the HLI dixies were nearly boiling, being licked by flames which illuminated the whole playground … presently the LRB arrived in driblets and enquired after their tepid dixies and, with their assistance, we endeavoured to make up for lost time. But most of them breakfasted that morning on bread and jam, followed by a second meal at 9 o'clock, consisting of a mug of tea and a rasher of smoky bacon. This was the first and last occasion on which I was appointed official cook.[127]

MANAGEMENT OF COOKHOUSES

The Sergt Cook should have a duty roster & detail his men for the cleaning up of the utensils, apparatus, etc and hold them responsible for the cleanliness of such. He should afford every facility in keeping the mess book, also see that there is a variety in the diet and see that there is no waste.

As far as possible food should be prepared for the following day, plenty of green-stuff should be recommended when in season.

He should be present at the issue of groceries, milk, etc and see that the proper quantities are received. He will also see that all meat in the ovens is properly turned about half way through the process of cooking and all stews frequently stirred. He will see that all utensils are hung up in their proper places, all boilers filled ready for use the next morning and fires laid. One boiler should be kept as a stock pot. All dripping should be kept in a dry, cool place. One man being told off to cook.

After this, if possible always try and keep a number of trained cooks. No washing or shaving to be allowed in cookhouse. No clothes etc to be hung about. Washing, shaving, smoking or drying of clothes is strictly forbidden in the kitchen either in barracks or in the field.

More usually, food in the United Kingdom was prepared in unit cook-houses. Here the cooking apparatus used were largely fuelled with coal, and the task of laying and stoking the fires and cleaning out ash was constant and backbreaking for some of the kitchen staff. The archaeological project at Belton House in Lincolnshire, the depot of the Machine Gun Corps from 1915, for the television series *Time Team*, produced lots of evidence from the various ash pits dotted around the site. Of particular interest was the excavation of one of the multiple cookhouses that produced evidence of pipe water, well-made drains and asbestos insulation.[128] The cooking appliances were variations of the type of cookers, boilers and ovens used in large-scale domestic cookery in hotels and other institutions. 'Warren's Improved Apparatus', for example, featured both an oven and boilers, as well as a variety of hot plates. 'Dean's Iron Oven' came in a variety of sizes, the largest of which could cook for 100 men.

'Dean's Steel Boilers' could prepare food for up to fifty men at a time and could be used for cooking meals or heating water for tea, although not both at the same time.[129] For this reason, a combined cooking apparatus was made available, with the 'Richmond Cooking Apparatus' consisting of 'oven and steam chambers, hot plate and boiler for generating steam, also providing water for tea and coffee' and a portion which consists of a 'soup and vegetable boiler and stock pot'.[130] Once again, this apparatus came in a choice of sizes: the smallest to cater for fifty men and the largest for 150 men. One surprising feature of this apparatus is the provision for cooking under pressure at a period well before the modern 'pressure cooker' came into domestic use. The final item detailed in the 1910 Manual is the 'Brick Oven'. This consisted of a circular brick chamber with a furnace fuelled by coal. Heating time varied from 1 to 2 hours, depending upon the quality of coal used. As there was no thermostat the manual indicates that the way to tell when the oven was up to temperature was to look through the hole in the oven door: 'If the soot is all burnt off the top and sides and the bricks have a bright red appearance, it is ready'. [131]

ARMY COOK'S TIP NO.15

Always bake bread in a very hot oven at first to mill the yeast and prevent the bread being full of holes and losing its shape.

From Log Book of G.N.R. Smith, 368 Siege Battery, RGA

One consequence of the Boer War was an obsession with hygiene. This resulted from the sickness and death rate during the conflict, largely due to drinking polluted water. Two-thirds of the deaths in the war resulted from ill health rather than enemy action, and this revolutionised the attitude towards sanitation in military camps. One of the features of British Army manuals after 1902 is the attention paid to cleaning waste water. One example of this is given in the 1918 Manual. The manual explains that it is possible to clear waste kitchen water of fats by means of a series old oil barrels as grease traps. This grease, it warns, 'blocks the drains' can be collected and 'sale of the grease is entirely for the benefit of the men' and that

'The country requires all available grease and fats for Munitions purposes'.[132] This illustrates the attention to detail demonstrated during the Great War to the recycling of materials for the war effort and the role that cooks played in the process. It is worth adding that they were expected to also recycle empty tins and even send back the skins of rabbits so that they could be made into fur gloves and jackets for the Royal Flying Corps.

KITCHEN RULES

1) Smoking strictly forbidden
2) Throwing fat bones or water on floor
3) Leaving water taps unattended when turned on
4) Leaving tables or bench dirty
5) Never clean utensils made of tin with sand but whiting
6) Never use cooking utensils for washing purposes
7) Sitting or lounging on tables
8) Leaving kitchen without permission
9) Taking any food except for testing purposes
10) Putting any articles on spare apparatus
11) Cleaning any apparatus on tables
12) Leaving sink dirty

From Pte C. Leveratt, No. 32880, 1 Garr. Batt., Worcester, Monkton Camp, Gosport; Cooking Course at Weymouth 3 August to 12 September 1916

CONCLUSION

TO JUDGE BY most popular accounts of the Great War, the rations received by British soldiers were at best a disaster and at worst a war crime. Even at the time, at least one serviceman suggested that the owner of the factory that manufactured Maconochies should have been shot. However, despite obvious and often reported shortcomings, the fact remains that, of the 908,371 deaths during the war,[133] only a tiny percentage can be attributed to diet. An analysis of casualties carried out for the *Official History of the British Army*[134] concluded that of a sample 1,043,653 casualties there were 1,987 cases of diseases of the teeth or gums; 11,480 cases of ulceration of the stomach; 5 cases of scurvy and 794 cases of alcoholism in all theatres of war. To put this in perspective, there was also 1,763 cases of sun stroke and 3,977 cases of burns or scalds.

In simple terms, soldiers did not starve and were not greatly weakened by malnutrition exposing them to diseases, as might be suggested by some accounts. This does not mean that the food was always good or adequate, only that for the majority of soldiers for most of the time it was sufficient, if not always to their liking. To achieve this requires a remarkable logistical effort combined with the preparation of millions of meals every day for a worldwide army. If you look simply at the task presented by feeding the British Expeditionary Force (BEF) in France and Flanders between 1914 and 1918 the numbers are staggering. By 11 November 1918, the BEF consisted of over 2⅓ million men and women. This is more than twice the modern population of Birmingham.[135] The big difference is not the numbers involved but the facilities required to feed these populations. Modern Birmingham lies at the centre of a road, rail and air network virtually at the centre of the United Kingdom. A system of depots, supermarkets and other distribution centres exists to provide food for domestic cooking or for the thousands of restaurants and takeaways, which supply the people with food on a daily basis. Most people are in a position to prepare their own food in kitchens intended to cook for a family, provided with the means to store food safely and hygienically, together with an area out of the elements to eat the finished product.

ARMY'S COOK TIP NO.16

To Cool an Oven

When an oven is too hot put a basin of cold water in it. This will reduce the temperature of the oven very quickly and the steam from the water will not inquire [sic] anything [that] is being cooked except puff pastry.

From Log Book of G.N.R. Smith, 368 Siege Battery, RGA

The BEF was on a foreign continent separated from Britain by sea. The majority of its members lived in camps, largely in rural areas where there had previously been no population centres before. This meant that the members of the BEF were at the furthest extent of railway supply routes, and some, those in the frontline, relied on horse power and even man-power to provide daily food. To complicate matters the means of cooking was a combination of a few central cooking depots or improvised cookers and ovens supplemented by, in emergency, whatever means was available to individual soldiers. There were few places where food could be stored for long periods, and enemy action, vermin and weather conditions all contributed to the difficulties encountered in getting food to where it was required. Even when this was achieved, its preparation to the satisfaction of the customers, the hungry soldier, was a gigantic, challenging and never-ending task. Whether a battle was being fought or prepared, on every day of the year, and in every imaginable weather condition, meals were presented for the members of the BEF. If some were tasteless, unimaginative or simply small, this cannot really surprise us.

As we have seen, food preparation presented a massive range of challenges, and we must recall that prior to the creation of the Army

Catering Corps in 1941, the responsibility for the supply of the rations and the training of the cooks fell to the Army Service Corps. The expansion of the army challenged all pre-war planning and turned tens of thousands of men from farmers and labourers to soldiers and cooks virtually overnight. There were protests over food in the British Army and a few mutinies, but unlike our allies, the French, these were never about shortage of rations.

All the above can be summed up in the words of the great historian of the British Army, in his foreword to the History of the Army Service Corps written in 1931:

> Altogether the achievements of the Army Service Corps in the late war strike me, who have followed pretty minutely the many campaigns of the British Army, as nothing short of marvellous. The Army of course would have been absolutely powerless without it. In the first place it was the Corps's representatives at the War Office, one and all of high professional calibre, who by keen foresight had made everything ready for the Expeditionary Force and by remarkable moral courage prevented any trouble over the food supply at home upon the opening of hostilities. In the second we find the spirit of imitative, acceptance of responsibility and readiness of improvisation pervaded the Corps in every sphere of operations. It mattered not whether the scene were the waterlogged plain of Flanders, or the mountains of Italy and Serbia, or the sands of Palestine, or the vast tropical jungle of East Africa, or the dreary banks of the Euphrates and Tigris, or the frost-bitten wastes of Archangel – whether on the equator or in the Arctic Circle – whether the thermometer stood at 120° Fahrenheit or at 50p below zero – whether there were roads or no roads – whether the approaches were safe or swept by shrapnel shell and machine-gun bullets – there was the Army Service Corps with but one governing brain, heart and limb – to keep the fighting men in good fettle for action or perish – as eight thousand did actually perish – in the attempt.[136]

A final acknowledgement for the task undertaken by the corps in the Great War came within one month of the Armistice. In December 1918, it became the Royal Army Service Corps – a designation and honour that reflected the contribution of the members of The Corps to victory.

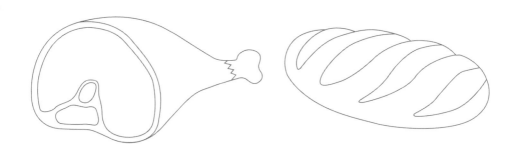

PART TWO

A COLLECTION OF TOMMY'S BATTLEFIELD RECIPES

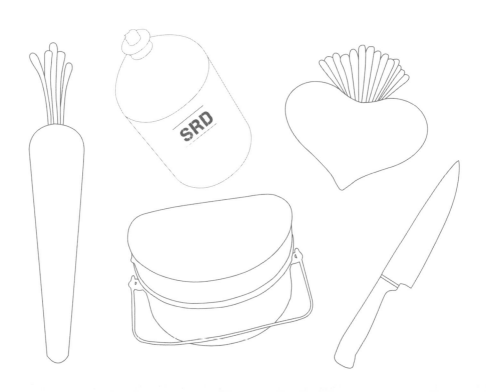

SOUPS AND STEWS

Pea Soup

Ingredients:

Split Peas	Pepper
Flour	Salt
Onions	Mint or Herbs
Mixed Vegetables	Stock

Method of Preparation:

- Soak the peas overnight.
- Bring the stock to the boil.
- Skin and cut-up the onions, wash peel and cut up vegetables into small pieces.
- Add peas, onions and mixed vegetable to the stock and boil till tender.
- Place flour, pepper and salt in a mixing bowl, add sufficient stock or water to make into thin paste and add to soup together with mint or herbs 30 minutes before required.

Hotch Potch Soup

Ingredients:

Mixed Vegetables	Mixed Herbs
Barley	Blue Peas
Lettuce	Stock
Onions	Flour
Parsley	Pepper & Salt

Method of Preparation:

- Soak the peas overnight.
- Seal the barley.
- Wash and peel the mixed vegetables and cut up into cubes.
- Clean and cut up onions.
- Wash and cut up lettuce into small pieces.
- Place sufficient stock in boiler, add the peas, barley, onions, lettuce and parsley, bring to a simmer till cooked.
- Bring soup to the boil, add thickening and herbs, keep well stirred for 30 mins and serve hot.
- Time 3½ to 4 hours.

Leek Soup

Ingredients:

Leeks
Rice
Parsley

Salt & Pepper
Stock

Method of Preparation:

- Cut away the roots and any discoloured parts from the leeks, cut in halves lengthways, then in thin slices, wash well, rinse and drain.
- Wash rice and add it with the leeks to the soup and boil slowly for 1 to 2 hours, skimming when necessary, simmer for 1 hour longer.
- Season to taste, add parsley and serve up.

Plain Stew

Ingredients:

Meat	Mixed Vegetables
Onions	Stock
Pepper	Flour
Salt	

Method of Preparation:

- Bone meat and remove the surplus fat, cutting up meat into pieces of about 1oz.
- Place a little stock into a cooking vessel, skin and cut up onions, wash and peel and cut up vegetables into small pieces.
- Place meat into vessel and add onions and mixed vegetables and well mix together, barely cover with stock and cook from 2½ to 3 hours.
- Place 3lb of flour, ½oz pepper, ½oz of salt into a bowl and mix well together, add sufficient cold water or stock to make into a smooth paste and add to stew 30 minutes before required.

Brown Stew

Ingredients:

Meat

Onions

Flour

Mixed Vegetables

Pepper

Salt

Stock

Method of Preparation:

- Bone meat, remove surplus fat, cut meat into 1oz pieces.
- Place 3lb flour, ½oz pepper, ½oz salt in a bowl and well mix together.
- Place a little stock into bottom of cooking vessel and dredge meat in flour.
- Peel and cut up onions, wash and peel and cut up the mixed vegetables, add onions and vegetables to meat, mix well together and barely cover with stock and place in over to cook.
- Stir frequently to prevent burning.
- Time 2½ to 3 hours.

Brown Curry Stew

Ingredients:

Meat	Flour
Mixed Vegetables	Pepper
Onions	Salt
Stock	Curry Powder

From Log Book of Pte C. Leveratt, 1916.

Method of Preparation:

- Cut meat in small cubes, taking away excess fat.
- Wash & peel & cut up veg.: peel & cut up onions.
- Place a small quantity of stock in baking dish.
- Place in mixed vegetables & onions.
- Place flour, pepper & salt, curry powder in mixing bowl, rub well together.
- Add meat & rub in untill [sic] it is all absorb [sic].
- Add this to mixed vegetables, stir well together, barely cover with stock.
- Cook in moderate oven, 2½ to 3 hours.
- Stirring & adding hot stock as necessary.
- Boiled Rice for Curry: first wash & pick over, remove all unhusked grains & sprinkle into boiling water to which salts is added boil untill [sic] tender, then strain.

Note:

A good way to cook large quantity of rice. As soon as you have added the rice to boiling water, remove or damp fire and allow to cook in own heat. Use plenty of water to boil in: 8 times the portion of water to 1 of rice. To test when done, pinch grain between thumb & finger, if no white remains it is cook[ed] enough.

Tomato Stew

Ingredients:

Meat

Onions

Tomatoes

Salt

Pepper

Flour

Stock

Method of Preparation:

- Bone meat and remove surplus fat, cut into 1oz pieces.
- Skin, clean and cut up onions.
- Place tomatoes in bottom of cooking vessel, add meat and well mix together, barely cover with stock and cook for 2½ to 3 hours.
- Place 3lb of flour, ½oz pepper, ½oz of salt into a bowl and mix well together, add sufficient cold water or stock to make into a smooth paste and add to stew 30 minutes before required.

Irish Stew

Ingredients:

Meat	Salt
Onions	Pepper
Potatoes	Stock

Method of Preparation:

- Remove the surplus fat and cut up meat into 1oz pieces.
- Skin and cut up the onions, wash, peel and rewash the potatoes.
- Place a little stock in the bottom of a cooking vessel then place a layer of potatoes in the bottom then a layer of meat.
- Sprinkle with onions, a little pepper and salt and add another layer of potatoes and so on until the vessel is three parts full, finishing off with a layer of potatoes.
- Barely cover with stock, replace lid and cook.
- Time 2½ to 3 hours.

VEGETABLES, ACCOMPANIMENTS & MEATLESS DISHES

TIME TO BOIL VEGETABLES

Carrots	60 minutes
Turnips	40 minutes
Cabbage	30 minutes
Green Peas (young)	10 minutes
Green Peas (old)	15 minutes
French Beans (young)	10 minutes
French Beans (old)	5 minutes
Sea Kale	15-20 minutes
Broccoli (small)	15 minutes
Broccoli (large)	25 minutes
Cauliflower (small)	15 minutes
Cauliflower (large)	25 minutes
Celery Stewed	25 minutes
Artichokes	20 minutes
Spinach	15 minutes
Veg. Marrow	20 minutes
Asparagrass [sic]	15 minutes
Onions	40 minutes
Beans	15 minutes

POTATOES

Potatoes are best when cooked in their skins but when it is necessary to peel them it should be done as thinly as possible as the best part of the potato is nearest the skin. After peeling they should be kept in cold water till required for use, if any be spotted in the inside they should be rejected as there [*sic*] flavour and the best part of there [*sic*] nutriment has been lost.

If for boiling a little salt should be dissolved in the water before the potatoes are placed in it. But it is better to steam them as their flavour is improved and the waste is less.

New potatoes should always be placed in boiling water with a little salt and not steamed.

Old potatoes should always be placed in boiling water with a little salt and not steamed. Old potatoes should always be placed in cold water.

Time for new 30 minutes. Old potatoes 40 minutes.

Substitutes for Potatoes

Bean Croquettes

Ingredients:

Beans (15lb)	Pepper & salt
Flour (2lb)	Stock or water

Method of Preparation:

- Soak the beans overnight in cold water, add 1½oz of soda.
- Boil the beans in stock or water until tender and the skins burst, drain and mash them.
- Add the flour and seasoning, mix well and make into shapes.
- Place them into baking dishes to cover the bottoms and bake in quick oven until brown.

Rice Croquettes

Ingredients:

Rice (10lb)
Flour (2lb)

Pepper & salt
Stock or water

Method of Preparation:

- Wash and rewash the rice, cook until tender in stock or water and drain, dredge in flour, season to taste and make into shapes.
- Place these into baking dishes with sufficient dripping to cover the bottoms and bake in quick oven until brown.

CARROTS

Carrots should always be sent up to the table with boiled beef, they vary much in quality but should be quite firm and have a crisp appearance when broken.

Young carrots should be washed and well scrubbed before cooking, old ones will require scraping and cutting into quarters length-ways, a little salt should always be cooked with them.

Savory Rice. Boiled to Serve with Hot Meat

Ingredients:

Rice (10lb)   Pepper & salt
Onions (2–6lb)   Stock or water
Dripping (1lb)

Method of Preparation:

- Wash and rewash the rice then plunge into 10 gallons of stock or water, cut up onions into small pieces, add them to the rice, season to taste with pepper and salt.
- When the rice is cooked and has absorbed all the water, add dripping and stir well.

PARSNIPS

Parsnips are served in a similar manner to carrots and are excellent for flavouring.

TURNIPS

Turnips can be used in all stews and should be mashed to flavour soups, after boiling they should be thoroughly strained. A little dripping, pepper and salt must be added to flavour and then mashed with an ordinary vegetable masher.

The turnips should be small, finely grained, juicy, smooth and round, and should be peeled as the part next to the skin is fibrous and indigestible.

(49)
Stuffed Tomatoes

Ingredient
Tomatoes cooked meat Bread crumbs Pepper Salt

method
mince meat up very fine cut off Top of Tomatoes scoop out inside mix it with minced meat Bread crumbs Pepper Salt Place it back in Tomatoes Place on Greased Baking Dish Cook in Moderate Oven for 10 minutes

note
They may be stuffed with a mixture made from grated cheese Bread crumb Pepper & Salt eggs mixed to a stiff Batter Then Bake in moderate Oven Could be served as Savoury Tomatoes Stuffed with Meat as an Entree or Savoury

From Log Book of Pte C. Leveratt, 1916.

Stuffed Tomatoes

Ingredients:

Tomatoes   Breadcrumbs
Cooked Meat   Pepper & Salt

Method of Preparation:

- Mince meat up very fine.
- Cut off top of tomatoes.
- Scoop out inside, mix it with minced meat, breadcrumbs, pepper & salt.
- Place it back in tomatoes.
- Place on greased baking dish.
- Cook in moderate oven for 10 minutes.

Note:

They may be stuffed with a mixture made from grated cheese, breadcrumbs, pepper & salt, eggs mixed to a stiff batter then bake in moderate oven. Could be served as savoury tomatoes stuffed with meat as an entrée or savoury.

ONIONS

This well known vegetable may be regarded either as a condiment or as an article of real nourishment, by boiling it is depriced of much of its pungent, volatile oil and becomes agreeable, mild and nutritious, as a light flavouring it is considered an improvement to many dishes.

Made in Stews and Pies, etc it will be found better to first place the onions in a little boiling water and soda and allowed to remain for ten minutes. The water will then be found quite green and should be thrown away as it contains the indigestible part of the onion.

Maccaroni Cheese

Ingredients:

Grated Cheese	Salt
Breadcrumbs	Butter
Maccaroni [sic]	If liked, flavour with Mustard
Pepper	

Method of Preparation:

- Boil macaroni [*sic*] till tender.
- Well grease shallow dish, sprinkle over breadcrumbs, grated cheese then place layer of macc [*sic*].
- Season with pepper & salt, mustard.
- Cover with breadcrumbs & cheese.
- Then another layer of maccaroni, continue till [*sic*] dish is full enough, having a layer of breadcrumbs on top.
- Place a piece of butter on the top, then place in moderate oven till nicely brown another way is to make white sauce by placing milk into saucepan.
- Bring to boil add a thickening made of flour, pepper, salt, milk.
- Allow to boil for few minutes, then add cheese which has been grated.
- Place boiled maccaroni in greased baking dish, pour over sauce, sprinkle breadcrumbs on top.
- Cook in moderate oven till nicely brown.

Another dish can be made with this sauce called **Cauliflower Cheese**.

Method of Preparation:

- Remove all green leafs [*sic*] from cauliflower.
- Wash in salt water.
- Place in boiling water to which salt & soda is added, boil gently till tender.
- Dish up on flat dish.
- Pour over sauce, sprinkle grated cheese
- Place in moderate oven for few minutes.
- Serve very hot.

Savoury

Ingredients:

Eggs
Milk
Mixed Herbs

Parsley
Onions if preferred

Method of Preparation:

- Break eggs into basin, add mixed herbs, pepper & salt.
- If using parsley or onions, chop very fine.
- Place in well battered pan.
- Place on hot plate, cook till set.
- Fold half way over & serve up on hot dish.

Note:

Little ham or tongue may be added, chopped very fine.

Curried Eggs Cold

Ingredients:

Hard Boiled Egg	Salt
Curry Powder	Butter
Pepper	Harvey or Worcester Sauce

Method of Preparation:

- Remove egg shells, cut in half, remove yoke & mix with curry powder, pepper, salt, flavouring of little sauce, small quantity butter.
- Place back into white of egg, serve up on thin buttered toast.
- These eggs may be done in same manner in using sardine or anchovies instead of curry powder, serving as Sardine Eggs.

French Eggs

- Take a small greased pot, spread with onions.
- Breaking egg & beat up, add pepper & salt.
- Place in oven till set & serve in pot cook[ed] in.

PIES

Potato Pie

Ingredients:

Meat	Pepper
Potatoes	Salt
Onions	Stock

Method of Preparation:

- Wash and peel and rewash potatoes, cutting large ones into halves lengthwise.
- Bone meat cutting away surplus fat, if meat is lean cover with slices of fat.
- Place potatoes in tin dish, peel and cut up onions and sprinkle over the potatoes add 1½oz pepper and 3oz of salt then pour over a little stock or water.
- Place dish in oven and turn joint at half time, add stock when necessary.
- Time 15 minutes to each lb of meat.

Meat Pie

Ingredients:

Meat	Flour
Onions	Baking Powder
Pepper	Cold Water
Salt	Dripping
Stock	

Method of Preparation:

- Cut meat in small cubes, taking away excess fat.
- Peel and cut up onions.
- Place a small quantity of stock in baking tin.
- Placing meat & onions in same.
- Season with pepper & salt.
- Stir well together, barely cover with stock.
- Place flour, baking powder & salt in mixing bowl.
- Rub well together to remove lumps.
- Shredd [sic] dripping if necessary, add to mix.
- Lightly make well in centre, add sufficient cold water to make a stiff dough.
- Turn out on well floured table, press out with both hands, turning over ends four times, picking up loose fragments & placing in centre.
- Turn paste over, cut into portion required, roll out to an even thickness and large enough to be able to take two strips from one side & one from the other & one from top, these stripps [sic] are for decoration purposes.
- Cut a hole in the centre to allow unwholesome gasses to escape.
- Place paste on meat, put stripps [sic] on.
- Cook in moderate oven for 2½ hours.

Note:

The pie to be placed on top shelf of oven to start to cook & brown paste then in cooler part of oven.

From Log Book of Pte C. Leveratt, 1916.

Sea Pie

Ingredients:

Meat	Stock
Potatoes	Flour
Onions	Baking Powder
Mixed Vegetables	Dripping
Pepper	Cold Water
Salt	

Method of Preparation:

• Cut meat in cubes, taking excess fat.
• Wash & peel & rewash potatoes.
• Peel and wash mixed vegetables.
• Peel & cut up onions.
• Place a small quantity of stock in cooking vessel.
• Place in meat, mixed vegetables, onions, potatoes on top, season with pepper & salt.
• Barely cover with stock then cover with paste made as for Meat Pie.
• Boil for 2½ to 3 hours, or they may be steamed.

FISH

Curried Cod

- Clean and cut up cod and cut into 4oz steaks.
- Place in cooking vessel and cover with water and cook until done, when done strain off water, keeping sufficient of the water that the fish has been boiled in
- Place flour, pepper, salt and curry powder in mixing bowl and mix well together.
- Add sufficient of the water to make into this paste, bring fish stock to the boil.
- Add thickening, cook for about 30 mins.
- Pour into dishes over cod and serve hot.

TIMES FOR COOKING FISH

BOILING

Brill	10 to 15 minutes
Cods Head & Shoulder	30 minutes
Cods Tail	20 minutes
Turbot (4 or 5lb)	30 minutes
Flounder	Simmer for 5 minutes
Haddock	20 minutes
Mackerell	10 minutes
Salmon	8 minutes per lb
Skate	45 minutes
Sole	10 minutes
Whiting	5 minutes

Note: Salmon to be put into hot water

FRYING

Cod Cutlets	5 to 10 minutes
Salmon Cutlets	5 to 10 minutes
Plaice	5 to 10 minutes
Sole	5 to 10 minutes
Skate	5 to 10 minutes

Soused Herrings

Ingredients:

Fish	Pepper
Onions	Salt
Cloves	Vinegar
Pepper Corns	Cold Water

Method of Preparation:

- Clean & gut fish, removing scales then leave in salt water 30 mins.
- Then place in baking dish, tail to tail.
- Sprinkle on onions which have been peel[ed] & cut up very fine.
- Add pepper corns, cloves, pepper, salt & the vinegar.
- Dilute with equall [sic] parts of cold water.
- Cook in moderate oven for 40 minutes.

Soused Mackerel

- Same method and ingredeint [sic] as above using Mackerel instead of Herrings.
- Dried Haddock
- Remove tail & finn [sic].
- Cut into pieces required.
- Place into dishes, pour over boiling water.
- Place in oven or on hot plate for 20 minutes.

Filletted [*sic*] Haddock

- It is best soaked in cold water then deal with as **Dried Haddock**.

Fresh Haddock

- Should be well washed & clean, then dipped in flour and fried in boiling fat till [*sic*] nicely brown.
- Kipper
- Place in baking tins, taking care they are all one way.
- Pour over boiling water then stand on hot plate or in oven for 20 minutes, or they may be steamed.

Dry Salted Fish

- Cut into pieces required.
- Soak in cold water 24 hours.
- Place in cold water and boil for 30 minutes.

Bloaters

- Place into greased baking dishes tail to tail.
- Cook in moderate oven 20 to 30 minutes or maybe grilled or fried.

Salt Wet Cod

- Boil in pieces or stakes [*sic*] or bake in oven.
- Place in cold water & bring steadily to boil for a few minutes then will be done.

Note:

Small quantity of vinegar to same amount of water, it is a great improvement to taste, when done it will crack on outside.

From Log Book of Pte C. Leveratt, 1916.

Salmon

- Place in boiling water, the testing of fresh by pressing with finger it will leave no impression. The gills are bright red & eyes forward & prominent. The spot on plaice and smelt should be bright red [sic].

Note:

The fish ration per man for dinner is ½lb. Serve with parsley sauce.

Ingredients:

Fish	Pepper
Stock	Salt
Milk	Parsley
Flour	

Method of Preparation:

- Wash & remove stock [sic] of parsley, chop up fine.
- Place a quantity of stock in boiler.
- Make a thickening of flour, pepper & salt.
- Add a little boiling stock & chopped parsley.
- Allow to simmer and keep well stirred for 10 minutes.
- This sauce can be made of all milk instead of stock.

Fish Cakes

Ingredients:

Cooked Fish or Tin Salmon   Pepper
Mashed Potatoes   Salt
White Breadcrumbs   Eggs
Parsley

Method of Preparation:

- Remove fish from bone, break into flakes.
- Wash parsley, remove stalk and chop up fine.
- Place all ingredeints [sic] except eggs in mixing bowl, mix well together.
- Break in eggs & mix well together.
- Shape into round shaped cakes.
- Place in greased baking dish.
- Cook in moderate oven till nicely brown.
- Time about 30 mins.

Note:

They may be fried in deep fat when you would paint over outside with eggs. Roll in flour and breadcrumbs. Place in boiling fat till nicely brown.

Fish Kedegree [*sic*]

Ingredients:

Cooked Fish   Salt
Rice   Eggs
Pepper

Method of Preparation:

- Bone fish, break in flakes.
- Boil rice untill [*sic*] tender.
- Boil egg for 10 minutes, remove shells.
- Place rice after strain.
- Fish, pepper, salt, white of eggs chopped up.
- Place into greased saucepan or cooking vessel.
- Place on hot plate till it becomes quite hot, keep stirring to prevent burning.
- Dish up on hot dish.
- Decorate with eggs chopped up small.

MEAT

MEAT INSPECTION

In beef the carcase externally should have a well filled and rounded appearance and well covered with bright, clean fat. Internally the chest and pelvic cavities and kidneys should be well covered with fat. The bones should be ruddy, porous and soft and plenty of cartilage should be visible on certain of them.

In mutton the same condition obtain to a certain degree.

The ox, heifer or cow fulfilling the condition of contract should be of medium confirmation as regards bone and general development.

The lean when cut should be bright and cherry colour. The pelvic cavity is wide and distended and the udder is brown, spongy and pendulous.

FROZEN MEAT

The meat is cold to the touch and particles of ice may be seen on cutting it with a saw, its colour is not so bright as that of some killed meat, when still frozen the carcase has externally a white appearance, the fat is also white distinct from the lean and rather crumbly. There are generally signs of rough handling and the outside is dirty and untidy.

When flawed the meat looks sodden, the fat is discoloured and the exterior of the carcase sweats considerably. In carcases of frozen meat the legs are bent towards the body.

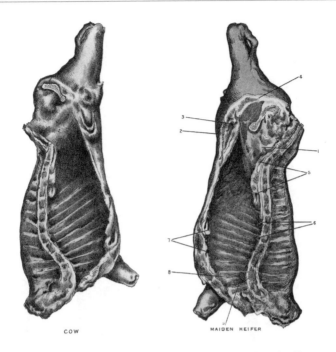

COW   MAIDEN HEIFER

Often military cooks had to be butchers too and were issued with all sorts of guidelines for checking the quality of meat:

A Guide to Carcass Meat

As it will be necessary under certain circumstances to make an examination of the glandular structures, the positions of the principal glands have been identified as follows:

1) Sacro-lumbar or iliae, found in the superficial fat at the junction of the rump and sirloin.
2) Super-inguinal, at the junction of the rump and thick flank.
3) Mammary group in the udder; in the ox these are absent, but he has instead the scrotal, to be found in the scrotal fat.
4) Deep inguinal or popliteal, to be found embedded in the fat of the silverside.
5) Lumbar group, to be found in the kidney fat near the vertebrae.
6) Dorso-corstal, close to the vertebrae, about the eighth and ninth ribs.
7) Sterno-costal, amongst the grisly termination of the true ribs.
8) Sub-scapular, embedded in fat between the scapula and first rib.
9) Super-sternal, in the superficial fat inside the first and second ribs.

In health glands should be of a brownish pink colour and gelatinous in appearance; but in cases of tuberculosis they become enlarged and loaded with grey matter, whilst in inflammatory complaints they become dark, congested, and haemorrhagic; they also afford early evidence of putrefactive change.

From the Instructions for the Guidance of Officers when Examining Fresh Meat (1910).

155

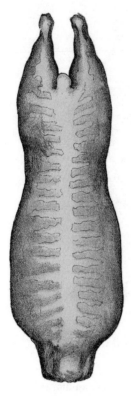
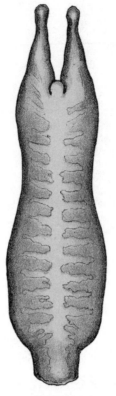

RAM   WETHER.

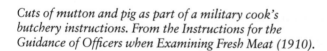

Cuts of mutton and pig as part of a military cook's butchery instructions. From the Instructions for the Guidance of Officers when Examining Fresh Meat *(1910).*

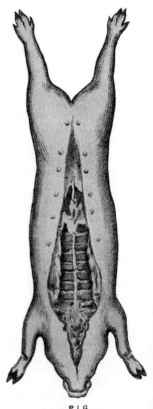

PIG

Stewed Steaks

Ingredients:

Meat	Flour
Onions	Pepper & salt
Mixed Vegetables	Dripping

Method of Preparation:

- Wash, cut up mixed vegetables into small pieces.
- Skin, clean and cut up the onions.
- Remove the meat from the bone and cut into 4oz steaks.
- Place a little dripping into the pan, add mixed vegetables and onions and fry till golden brown colour.
- Remove them quickly and brown steaks on both sides.
- Mix flour, salt and pepper, add to remaining fat in the pan and stir until all the fat is absorbed, then add hot water until the amount of gravy is obtained.
- Place the gravy into a dish, add the fried vegetables and onions between the steaks.
- Place the dish in oven or on hot plate till tender.
- Time 2 hours

Meat Rissoles and Gravy

Ingredients:

Meat	Bread	Mixed Herbs
Suet	Onions	
Flour	Pepper & Salt	

Method of Preparation:

- Bone the meat and cut into small cubes.
- Skin the suet and chop up finely.
- Skin, clean and cut up the onions.
- Remove the crust from the bread and soak in cold water for a few minutes, squeeze the water out of the bread and crumble into a mixing bowl.
- Place in the other ingredients and mix well together, then pass the whole through a mincer.
- Add sufficient flour to bind.
- Mould into sausage shapes, put into well greased tins and place into moderate heated ovens to cook.
- Place sufficient stock in boiler.
- Place flour, salt and pepper in mixing bowl.
- Add sufficient stock or water to make into a smooth, thin paste, add this to stock to make a nice thick gravy.
- Remove rissoles from oven when 3 parts cooked and partly cover with gravy and and replace in oven to finish.
- Time about 45 minutes

SWEETNESS OF MEAT

To decide whether the meat is sweet or tainted, the senses of taste and smell must be employed. Fresh meat is slightly acid to the taste while stale meat is distinctly alkaline, if there is any doubt the meat should be probed at its thickest portions with a clean wooden skewer, well thrusting, if possible, close to the bone and the skewer quickly withdrawn and smelt.

Boiled Beef and Carrots

Ingredients:

Beef	Flour	Stock or Water
Carrots	Pepper & Salt	

Method of Preparation:

- Roll, bone and skewer the meat.
- Place sufficient water in the boiler to cover the meat, bring to the boil, add 2oz of salt and the meat and boil hard for about ten minutes then reduce to a simmer.
- In the meantime wash, scrape and cut up the carrots into quarters and add to the boiler containing the beef, leaving till cooked. Time 18 minutes per lb.
- Remove the meat when ready and carve up thinly, then remove the carrots from boiler.
- Place flour, pepper and salt into a mixing bowl to make a thickening, add to the water that the meat and carrots have been cooked in, then cover the carved meat with the gravy and keep hot until required to serve.

THE SHEEP OF MUTTON – FIELD COOKING

On service it may be found necessary for troops to secure and butcher their own meat ration, the following is a rough guide for such work. When cut up for issue, the joints are as follows:

1) Scrap End for boiling or stewing.
2) Best End of neck can be baked or cut into chops, and fried and stewed.
3) Shoulders should be baked or roasted or can be boned, rolled and stuffed and roasted.
4) Breast can be rolled and baked or stewed.
5) Loin can be baked or roasted in one piece or may be cut into chops and stewed.
6) Legs may be roasted, baked, or boiled.

Stewed Kindney [*sic*] (Sheeps)

Method of Preparation:

- Cut in half, removing skin then fry till nicely brown.
- Place into stew pan.
- Place a little flour into fat fried in, season with pepper & salt.
- Rub in till all absord [*sic*].
- Add a little stock, make into thick gravy, keeping well stirred.
- Pour this over kidneys & stew for about 1½ hours.

Devilled Kidney

- Make a few incessions [*sic*] in kidney.
- Place into incessions pepper & salt, the flavouring of sauce.
- Grill for a few minutes in front of fire or fry.
- Best grilled.

Boiled Bacon

- Soak for a few hours, then place in boiling water, allow to rapidly boil for 10 min.
- Then reduce to simmer.
- If ham [h]as not been soaked start to cook in cold water to extract the salt.
- Time for cooking 15 to18 minutes per lb.
- It is an improvement to the ham to allow to cook in liquor boiled in.
- Taking care not to over boil as it will cook a certain amount while cooling.
- To test if done take a corner of rind, if it comes away from fat clean & easy it is done.
- The small bone of knuckle will be loose if ham is cooked.

Fried Liver and Onions

Ingredients:

Liver	Pepper
Onions	Salt
Flour	Dripping

Method of Preparation:

- Cut liver into thin slices.
- Peel & cut up onions into rings.
- Place flour, pepper, salt in mixing bowl.
- Add liver, rub in till absorb [*sic*], then place into boiling fat, taking care to have one layer, keep moving to prevent burning.
- Fry onions till [*sic*] nicely brown, add sprinkle over liver.
- Add a little stock and serve up after pouring away any excess fat.

Note:

May be cooked in greased baking tins or Aldershot Ovens & other kinds. When you don't rub liver in dry flour, make a thick gravy to serve up with. If you have a large quantity of onions to fry a good plan is to boil then fry them.

Meat Croquettes

Ingredients:

Minced Meat (cooked)	Baking Powder
Onions	Dripping
Parsley	Cold Water
Pepper	Eggs
Salt	Breadcrumbs
Flour	

Method of Preparation:

- Make light flakey paste, roll out thinly as possible.
- Mix minced meat & seasoning together.
- Place in paste, shape into round pattees, making sure edges are stuck by damping then with cold water.
- Paint over with egg, roll in breadcrumbs.
- Fry in deep fat till nicely brown dish upon white paper or greased to move.

(52)
Meat Croquette
Ingredeint
    minced Meat (cooked) Onions
Parsly Pepper Salt Flour Baking Powder
Dripping Cold Water Eggs Bread
crumbs
Method
    make light & flakey Paste roll
out as thinly as Possible mix minced
Meat & seasoning Together Place
in Paste shape into round Pattees
making sure Edges stuck by Damping
them with Cold Water Paintover
with Egg roll in Bread Crumbs
Fry in deep Fat till nicely brown
Dish upon White Paper or Greased to
move)

CAKES, BREAD & PUDDINGS

Making Cakes

Ingredients for Plain Cake:

Flour	Currants
Carbonate of Soda	Sugar
Cream Tarta	Dripping
Salt	Milk

Method of Preparation:

- Cream tarta & salt in mixing bowl.
- Rub well together if possible pass through fine seive [*sic*].
- Wash & pick over currants.
- Shredd dripp. & add to flour & well rub in untill it resemble breadcrumbs, add currants & mix well together.
- Add milk, well mix into stiff batter.
- Place into greased baking tin lard or dripping is best about 2 inches thick.
- Cook in moderate oven for 1 hour.
- To test if done, peirced [*sic*] with clean knife if it comes out clean it is done.

Flying Ferment

Simple way to make bread termed flying ferment.

Ingredients:

Flour	Yeast
Salt	Water

Method of Preparation:

- Shift [sic] flour, make well in centre.
- Mix up yeast, quite smooth.
- Add a little more than one third of water then mix up yeast with small quantity between 90 to 100 degrees hot water.
- Stir in enough flour to make a thin batter, stand aside till fit to work.
- Keep in warm temperature free from draft.
- Allow to stand 1½ hours when worked enough.
- Dissolve salt in remainder of water, same temperature as first used.
- Well break up yeast.
- Place into flour, add water & dough well kneaded.
- Stand aside for 2 hours to prove.
- When risen enough take out, cut into portions of 2lb, 20oz.
- Mould into shape.
- Place in slightly greased tins, allow to rise then cook in moderate oven 1 hr (that is for a 2lb loaf: 20lb flour, 40oz yeast, 40oz salt, 1 gallon of water make about twelve loaves)

Bread and Butter Pudding

Ingredients:

Bread
Currants
Sugar
Milk

Suet
Margarine
Nutmeg

Method of Preparation:

- Place thin layer of bread and butter on bottom of greased baking dish, sprinkle over with currants and well chopped suet, also sugar then so on until dish is 3 parts full then cover with milk and grate over with nutmeg.
- Time to cook 1 hour.

Tapioca Pudding

Ingredients:

Tapioca	Milk	Nutmeg
Sugar	Butter	

Method of Preparation:

- Soak tapioca for 3 hours then mix the tapioca, milk and sugar well together, and place in greased baking dish.
- Add butter or margarine in small lumps and grate over with nutmeg and place in the oven to brown, and then remove to cooler part of the oven to cook through thoroughly.

Ground Rice Pudding (for 100 men)

Ingredients:

Ground Rice (10lb)	Water (5 pints)	Custard (½lb)
Milk (10 pints)	Sugar (4lb)	Nutmegs (2)

Method of Preparation:

- Bring water and milk to the boil.
- Stir the rice in sharply.
- Place the mixture into a greased pan.
- Break the butter into small pieces, place on top with nutmegs grated on top and place in hot oven to brown.

Milk Biscuit Pudding (for 100 men)

Ingredients:

Biscuits (15lb)
Milk (3lb or 3 Tins)
Sugar (5lb)

Currants (4lb)
Spice (1 Packet)
Candied Peel (4oz)

Method of Preparation:

- Soak biscuits until soft, about 3 hours in cold water.
- Wash and pick over the currants, cut up peel finely.
- Place biscuits, sugar and currants into baking dishes.
- Add milk and mix well together with spice & peel and place in oven till cooked.
- Time 1 hour.

Lemon Pudding

Method of Preparation:

- Soak biscuits till soft.
- Then pass them thoroughly through a mincer.
- Mix biscuits, sugar, dripping & lemon into a stiff paste.
- Add flour to bind, cut into portions and place into floured cloths or greased dishes and steam or boil.
- Time 2½ hours.

Jam Roll

Ingredients:

Flour
Baking Powder
Salt

Dripping
Cold Water

Method of Preparation:

- Make paste as for meat pie.
- Cut in portions required, roll out to even thickness, keeping as square as possible.
- Spread on jam within an inch of edges.
- Damp same with cold water, roll towards you, pressing in edges to keep jam from boiling out.
- Place on damp floured cloth, roll up & tie each end with string in bows.
- Plunge into boiling water. Boil for 3 to 4 hours, adding boiling water as required.

Maccaroni Pudding

Ingredients:

Maccaroni [*sic*]   Nutmeg
Sugar   Salt
Milk   Water
Butter

Method of Preparation:

- Break into pieces about 1 inch.
- Place in boiling water, salt added.
- Then boil gently till [*sic*] tender.
- Strain off and place in baking dish.
- Add sugar & milk.
- Stir well together, put on peices [*sic*] of butter.
- Grate on nutmeg.
- Cook in moderate oven for 40 minutes till [*sic*] brown.

Note:

It should be boiled very gently, use plenty of water to allow to expand.

Apple Charlotte

Method of Preparation:

- Grease baking dish.
- Place slices of bread & butter in bottom & sides, then place stewed apples in.
- Cover the apples with bread & butter, taking care apples are covered, then sprinkle a little sugar on top.

Note:

A **Friar Omelette** is made with breadcrumbs instead of slices.

Apple Tarts

Ingredients:

Apple Rings	Salt
Cloves & Sugar	Dripping
Flour	Cold Water
Baking Powder	

Method of Preparation:

- Soak apple rings overnight in cold water.
- Place in baking dish, add sugar & cloves with small quantity of cold water.
- Place in dish, cover with light flakey [sic] paste.
- Cook in moderate oven for 1½ to 2 hours.

Chocolate Shape for 100 men

Ingredients:

Corn Flour,   1 Chocolate Powder
Sugar (4lb)   Milk (6 Tins)

Note:

Place corn flour, chocolate powder, sugar in milking bowl.
Make into smooth batter, add boiling water. Keep well stirred till [*sic*] it thickens, then place in ration tins till set.

Coffee Shape for 100 men

Ingredients:

Corn Flour   Milk
Liquid Coffee (1 Pint)   Sugar

Method of Preparation:

• Place corn flour in mixing bowl, add coffee & milk.
• Make into smooth batter, made same as chocolate shape.

Sweet Omelette

Ingredients:

Eggs   Butter
Milk   Caster Sugar
Jam

Method of Preparation:

- Break eggs in basin.
- Well beat with sugar & milk.
- Place in hot buttered pan, pour in mixture.
- Place on hot plate till set.
- When quite set and browning underneath.
- Place jam over half & fold the other half, cook over.
- Dish up on hot dish.

Note:

Omelette should never be turned. Equal quantity of eggs & milk to be used.

SAUCES

SAUCES TO BE SERVED WITH MEATS

Roast Beef	Horseradish Sauce
Grilled Stake [*sic*]	Mushroom or Tomatoes
Roast Mutton	Red Currant, Brown Caper Sauce
Boiled Mutton	Parsley or Caper
Grilled or Fried Chops	Tomato
Roast Pork	Apple Sauce
Pork Cutlets	Mustard Sauce
Boiled Ham	Parsley Sauce
Roast Lamb	Mint Sauce

Melted Butter Sauce

Ingredients:

Milk or Water	Flour
Butter	

Method of Preparation:

- Place the butter in a pan and allow to become hot, then add sufficient flour to absorb it. Have the milk or water hot and add it to the flour and butter, stir well until it comes to the boil.
- Then allow to cook until a nice creamy substance is obtained.
- Time 15 minutes.

Caper Sauce

Ingredients:

Melted Butter

Capers

Vinegar

Salt & Pepper

Method of Preparation:

- Place the butter into a pan until it becomes hot, add to it caper, vinegar, salt & pepper.
- And use as required. If for serving with boiled mutton, make the butter sauce with the water in which the meat was boiled in.

Onion Sauce

Ingredients:

Milk (½ pint)   Butter (1oz)   Pepper & Salt
Flour (1oz)   Onions (½lb)

Method of Preparation:

- Clean the onions and boil till tender.
- Chop up coarsely.
- Place the butter in a pan, allow to be melted. Add the flour and stir for a few minutes then add the milk and stir until it boils.
- Add the onions, season with pepper and salt and allow to simmer for a few minutes.
- Time 1½ hrs.

Sweet Sauce

Ingredients:

Milk   Sugar   Salt
Butter   Flour

Method of Preparation:

- Make the melted butter sauce.
- Add sugar and a pinch of salt, simmer for 5 minutes then serve.
- Time 20 minutes.

White Sauce for Puddings

Ingredients:

Milk (¾ pint)   Sugar
Corn Flour (1 desert spoon)   Pinch Salt
Lemon Rind (2 or 3 strips)

Method of Preparation:

- Blend the Corn Flour smoothly with a little milk and place the remainder in a pan.
- Add the lemon rind and salt.
- Simmer for 10 or 15 minutes then strain over the blended Corn Flour stirring well, return to the pan.
- Sweeten to taste and cook gently for 5 minutes, any flavouring may be used instead of Lemon Rind.
- Time 20 minutes.

White Sauce for Vegetables

Ingredients:

Butter	Milk	Bay Leaf
Flour	Stock	Salt & Pepper

Method of Preparation:

- Melt the butter in a pan, stir in the flour and cook for a few minutes, but don't allow to brown.
- Add the milk and stir until it boils, then add the stock and bayleaf and allow to simmer for 15 minutes.
- Remove bayleaf, season to taste and strain.
- Time 30 minutes

Mint Sauce

Ingredients:

Chopped Mint	Vinegar	Sugar

Method of Preparation:

- Young and fresh gathered mint is best, wash it free from grit, pick the leaves from the stalks and chop it finely.
- Place into a dish, add the sugar and vinegar and stir until the sugar is dissolved.
- This sauce should be made 2 or 3 hours before being required.

Custard Sauce (for 100 men)

Ingredients:

Custard Powder (1½lb)   Milk (12 pints)
Sugar (2lb)   Water (12 pints)

Method of Preparation:

- Mix milk and water to mix custard into thin paste.
- Bring the milk to the boil, stirring in the sugar and re-boil.
- Stir in sharply the custard mixture and allow to remain until boiling point is reached again, stirring continually.

From Log Book of Pte C. Leveratt, 1916.

(54)

Making. Tea: Coffee. Cocoa

Tea for 20 men

Place 2 Handsfull of Tea in Pail. Pour over Boiling water Sufficient for when Milk is added it just reaches Lip of Pail Allow to Draw 4 minutes Then strain add milk & Sugar mixed

note

If making tea in fixed Boilers care to be taken that it dont boil after tea is added If using muslin bag never tie tight Making Tea in Camp Kettle on Trench Fire remove Kettle as soon as Tea is Put in never add tea before Water Boils

Coffee

method

Place clean dry vessel Pour in over Boiling Water allow to stand till all strength is

(55)

extracted Then add sugar & Hot Milk then serve

Cocoa

method

Cocoa Should be mixed in small quanity of Milk or Water to thin Paste then add Boiling Water & Sugar & Milk

note

Cocoa is improved by Boiling a few minutes to bring out Flavour All prepared cocoa is directed on Tins If using Ships cocoa it should be broken up small. Soaked overnight in Small quanity of Water In the morning add boiling Water and Boil for 30 minutes

MAKING TEA, COFFEE, COCOA

TEA FOR 20 MEN

Place 2 handsfull [sic] of tea in pail.
Pour over boiling water.
Sufficient for when milk is added it just reaches lip of pail.
Allow to draw 4 minutes then strain.
Add milk & sugar mixed.

NOTE:

If making tea in fixed boilers care to be taken that it don't boil after tea is added. If using muslin bag never tie tight. Making tea in camp kettle on trench fire, remove kettle as soon as tea is put in, never add tea before water boils.

COFFEE

METHOD OF PREPARATION:

Place in clean, dry vessel.
Pour over boiling water.
Allow to stand till all strength is extracted then add sugar & hot milk the serve.

COCOA

METHOD OF PREPARATION:

Cocoa should be mixed in small quantity of milk or water to thin paste. Then add boiling water & sugar & milk.

NOTE:

Cocoa is improved by boiling a few minutes to bring out flavour.
All prepared cocoa is directed on tins.
If using Ships cocoa it should be broken up small. Soaked overnight in small quantity of water. In the morning add boiling water and boil for 30 minutes.

All recipes in this section are taken directly from Army Cooks' log and recipe books from 1914–18, courtesy of The Royal Logistic Corps Museum.

SELECT BIBLIOGRAPHY

Official Publications and Manuals

Beadon, Colonel R.H., *The Royal Army Service Corps, A History Of Transport And Supply In The British Army, Vol. II* (Cambridge University Press, 1931)

Becke, Major A. F., *Order of Battle Of Divisions, Part 3, New Army Divisions* (9–26) (The Naval and Military Press Ltd, 2007)

Edmonds, Brigadier-General Sir James E. (ed.), *Military Operations: France and Belgium, 1917* (HMSO, 1940)

Field Service Manual 1914 (HMSO, 1914)

Forbes, Major General A., *A History of the Army Ordnance Corps, Vol. 3: The Great War* (The Medici Society, 1922)

Hospital Ready Reckoner, Giving A Complete Scale Of The Diets For Patients in Military Hospitals (HMSO, 1914)

MacPherson, Major-General Sir W. G. (ed.), *History Of The Great War: Medical Services, Hygiene Of The War, Vol. II* (HMSO, 1923)

Manual of Military Cooking 1910 (HMSO, 1910)

Manual of Military Cooking and Dietary, 1918 (HMSO, 1918)

Mitchell, Major T.J., and Miss G. M. Smith, *History of The Great War. Medical Services, Casualties and Medical Statistics* (HMSO, 1931)

Standing Orders of an Infantry Battalion (Hugh Rees Ltd, 1917)

Statistics of The Military Effort Of The British Army During The Great War, 1914–20 (The War Office, 1922)

Personal Accounts

Coppard, George, *With A Machine Gun To Cambrai* (Cassell and Co., 1980)

Dent, Olive, *A V.A.D. in France* (Grant Richards, 1917)

Dolden, A. Stuart, *Cannon Fodder: an Infantryman's Life On The Western Front 1914–18* (Blandford Press, 1980)

Jackson, John, *Private 12768: Memoir of a Tommy* (Tempus, 2004)

Rifleman, A., *Four Years on the Western Front* (Oldham's Press, 1922)

Springer, S., and A. Humphreys (ed.), *Private Beatson's War: Life, Death and Hope On The Western Front* (Pen and Sword, 2009)

St Clair, William, (ed. John St Clair) *The Road to St Julien: The Letters of a Stretcher-Bearer from the Great War* (Leo Cooper, 2004)

Cook's Log Books

Private A. Flitney, RLC Museum

Corporal P. R. Froud, RLC Museum

Private C. Leveratt, RLC Museum

Other Publications

Brophy, J., and Eric Partridge, *The Daily Telegraph Dictionary of Tommies' Songs and Slang, 1914–18* (Frontline Books, 2008)

Forbes CB, CMG, Major General A., *A History of the Army Ordnance Corps, Vol. 3: The Great War* (Medici Society, 1929)

NOTES

1 *Blackadder Goes Forth*, 1989.
2 Rifleman, A., *Four Years on the Western Front* (Oldham's Press, 1922) p.97.
3 Coppard, G., *With A Machine Gun to Cambrai* (Cassell and Co., 1980) p.45.
4 Springer, S. and S. Humphreys (ed.), *Private Beatson's War: Life, Death and Hope on the Western Front* (Pen and Sword, 2009) p.72.
5 Coppard, p.85.
6 *Four Years on the Western Front*, p.51.
7 *Ibid*, p.66.
8 Brophy, J., and E. Partridge, *The Daily Telegraph Dictionary of Tommies' Song and Slang, 1914–18* (Frontline, 2008) p.27.
9 Coppard, p.56.
10 *Ibid*, p.43.
11 *Four Years on the Western Front*, p.97.
12 Coppard, pp.44–54.
13 Jackson, J., *Private 12768: Memoir of a Tommy* (Tempus, 2004) p.160.
14 Dolden, A., *Cannon Fodder: An Infantryman's Life on the Western Front, 1914–18* (Blandford Press, 1980) p.99.
15 *Private Beatson's War*, p.75.
16 *Ibid*, p.67.
17 Forbes CB, CMG, Major General A., *A History of the Army Ordnance Corps, Vol. 3: The Great War* (Medici Society, 1929).
18 Ration Strength: 11 Nov 18, France and Flanders: 2,360,400 men and women and 404,000 animals. Total worldwide: 5,363,352 and 895,700 animals. 'Statistics of the Military Effort of The British Empire during the Great War, 1914–18' (War Office, 1922) p.29.
19 *Ibid*, p.76.
20 *Ibid*.
21 Cole, Howard N., *The Story of the Army Catering Corps and Its Predecessors* (Army Catering Corps Association: 1984) p.13.
22 Cole, p.13.
23 Cowen, Ruth, *Relish: The Extraordinary Life of Alexis Soyer Victorian Celebrity Chef* (Phoenix, 2006).

24 Cole, p.21.
25 *Ibid*, p.27.
26 Wyndham, Horace, *The Queen's Service* (1899); Cole, p.39.
27 Cole, p.40.
28 Young, Michael, *Army Service Corps, 1902–1918* (Leo Cooper, 2000) p.385.
29 Beadon, Col R.H., *The Royal Army Service Corps: A History of Transport and Supply in the British Army, Vol. II* (Cambridge University Press, 1931) p.xxxiv.
30 Select Committee on Physical Deterioration, 1904.
31 Francis George Heath, P.S., *British Rural Life and Labour* (King and Son, 1911) p.69.
32 Cole, p.32.
33 *Ibid*, pp.32–33.
34 Dolden, p.64.
35 Attestation Paper in Pension Record. The National Archives, Kew.
36 Private C. Leveratt's Log Book, RLC Museum.
37 Manual of Military Cooking, 1910 (HMSO, 1910) p.22.
38 *Ibid*, p.25.
39 *Ibid*, p.12.
40 *Ibid*, p.12.
41 Log Book of Cpl P.R. Froud, RLC Museum.
42 Manual of Military Cooking, 1910 (HMSO, 1910) pp.13–14.
43 *Ibid*, pp.16–17.
44 Standing Orders of an Infantry Battalion (Hugh Rees Ltd, 1917) pp.42–43.
45 *Ibid*, p.109.
46 Log Book of Cpl P. R. Froud, RLC Museum.
47 *Ibid*.
48 St Clair, William (ed. John St Clair), *The Road to St Julien: The Letters of a Stretcher-Bearer from the Great War* (Leo Cooper, 2004).
49 Statement of Service in Pension Record. The National Archives, Kew.
50 Dolden, pp.95–96.
51 *Ibid*, p.79.
52 *Ibid*, p.81.
53 *Four Years on the Western Front*, p.55.
54 Dolden, p.69.
55 *Ibid*, p.158.
56 *Ibid*, p.147.
57 *Ibid*, p.106.
58 *Ibid*, p.151.
59 1911 Census.
60 Medal Index Card at the National Archives, Kew.
61 Archive of the RLC Museum, Deepcut, Surrey. RLCA 8278.
62 Coppard, p.44.
63 Becke, Major A.F., *Order of Battle Of Divisions, Part 3, New Army Divisions (9–26)* (The Naval and Military Press Ltd, 2007).
64 Edmonds, Brigadier-General Sir James E. (ed.), *Military Operations: France and Belgium, 1917* (HMSO, 1940).
65 Website of the Commonwealth War Graves Commission.

66 Archive of the RLC Museum.
67 Francis, p.65.
68 *Ibid.*
69 Macpherson, Major-General Sir W.G., (ed.) *History of the Great War: Medical Services, Hygiene of the War, Vol. II* (HMSO, 1923) pp.2, 4–11.
70 *Ibid*, pp.6–11.
71 A.B.14: 'Ready Reckoner for Field Rations'.
72 *Ibid*, pp.46–47.
73 *Ibid*, pp.46–47.
74 *Ibid*, pp.46–47.
75 Cole, p.59.
76 Young, p.50.
77 Beadon, p.48.
78 *Ibid*, p.94.
79 *Ibid*, p.48.
80 *Ibid*, p.49.
81 *Ibid*, diagram between pp.154 and 155.
82 Field Service Manual, 1914 (HMSO, 1914) p.54.
83 *Ibid*, p.51.
84 'Handbook Specifications for Supplies, 1915', p.7.
85 Coppard, p.43.
86 Macpherson, p.43.
87 Beadon, p.63.
88 Beadon, Col R.H., *The Royal Army Service Corps A History of Transport and Supply in the British Army, Vol II*, p.89.
89 Coppard, p.42.
90 'Handbook Specifications for Supplies, 1915', p.6.
91 Coppard, p.43.
92 *Ibid*, p.42.
93 *Four Years on the Western Front*, p.209.
94 *Ibid*, p.210.
95 *Ibid*, p.55.
96 *Ibid*. p.45.
97 *Ibid*.
98 Springer, S., and S. Humphreys (ed.), *Private Beatson's War: Life, Death and Hope On The Western Front* (Pen and Sword, 2009) p.76.
99 *Beatson's War*, p.85.
100 *Ibid*, p.66.
101 Dent, Olive, *A V.A.D. in France* (Grant Richards, 1917) pp.302–03.
102 *Ibid*, p.303.
103 *Four Years on the Western Front*, p.250.
104 Manual of Military Cooking, 1910 (HMSO, 1910) p.59.
105 Manual of Military Cookery and Dietary, 1918 (HMSO, 1918) p.A2
106 Manual of Military Cooking, 1910 (HMSO, 1910) p.63.
107 *Ibid*, p.63.
108 *Ibid*, p.63.
109 *Four Years on the Western Front*, p.157.

110 Macpherson, p.51.
111 Brown, Malcolm, *Tommy Goes to War* (Dent, 1978) p.75.
112 Dolden, p.108.
113 *Ibid*, p.151.
114 *Ibid*, p.108.
115 Macpherson, p.51.
116 Macpherson, p.51.
117 Field Service Manual, 1914 (HMSO, 1914).
118 Manual of Military Cooking and Dietary, 1918 (HMSO, 1918).
119 Cole, p.21.
120 Manual of Military Cooking, 1910 (HMSO, 1910) pp.59–63.
121 *Ibid*, p.60.
122 *Ibid*, p.61.
123 *Ibid*, p.60.
124 *Ibid*, pp.64–65.
125 'Statistics'. pp.842–43.
126 Manual of Military Cooking, 1910 (HMSO, 1910) p.66.
127 *Four Years on the Western Front*, pp.8–9.
128 *Time Team*, Channel 4, November 2012.
129 Manual of Military Cooking, 1910 (HMSO, 1910) pp.3–6.
130 *Ibid*, pp.7–8.
131 *Ibid*, p.9.
132 Manual of Military Cooking and Dietary, 1918 (HMSO, 1918) p.122.
133 'Statistics', p.237.
134 Mitchell, Major T.J., and Miss G.M. Smith, *History of The Great War. Medical Services, Casualties and Medical Statistics* (HMSO, 1931) pp.286–294.
135 1,036,900. Office of National Statistics 2012.
136 Beadon, pp.xlviii–xlix.

If you enjoyed this book, you may be interested in...

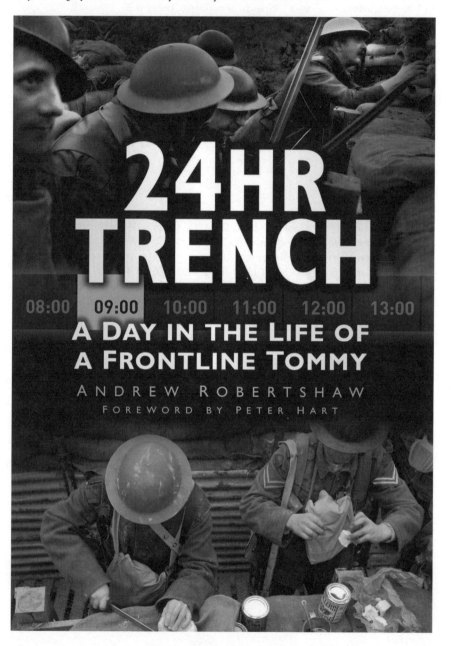

24HR TRENCH

08:00　09:00　10:00　11:00　12:00　13:00

**A DAY IN THE LIFE OF
A FRONTLINE TOMMY**

ANDREW ROBERTSHAW

FOREWORD BY PETER HART

9780752476674; £14.99

FRONTLINE COOKBOOK

BATTLEFIELD RECIPES FROM THE SECOND WORLD WAR

ED. ANDREW ROBERTSHAW

IN ASSOCIATION WITH THE
ROYAL LOGISTIC CORPS MUSEUM

9780752476650; £12.99

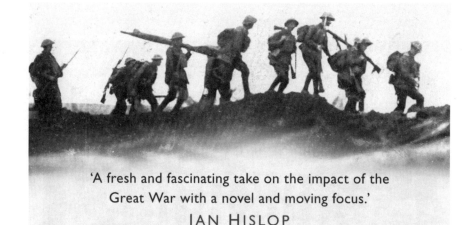

'A fresh and fascinating take on the impact of the
Great War with a novel and moving focus.'
IAN HISLOP

THE FINAL
WHISTLE

THE GREAT WAR
IN FIFTEEN PLAYERS

STEPHEN COOPER

FOREWORD BY BILL BEAUMONT CBE, DL

Shortlisted for the British Sports Book Awards, 2013
9780752499000; £9.99

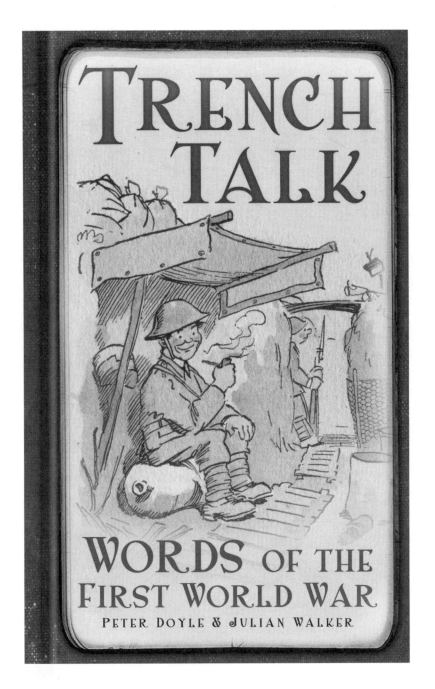

TRENCH TALK

WORDS OF THE FIRST WORLD WAR

PETER DOYLE & JULIAN WALKER

9780752471549; £9.99

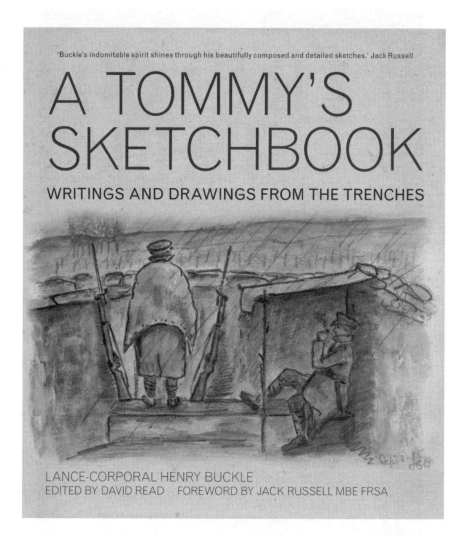

'Buckle's indomitable spirit shines through his beautifully composed and detailed sketches.' Jack Russell

A TOMMY'S SKETCHBOOK

WRITINGS AND DRAWINGS FROM THE TRENCHES

LANCE-CORPORAL HENRY BUCKLE
EDITED BY DAVID READ   FOREWORD BY JACK RUSSELL MBE FRSA

9780752466057; £9.99

Visit our website and discover thousands of other History Press books.

www.thehistorypress.co.uk